Strange New Country

To my good friend Dennis Brown

Konaway tillicums klatawa kunamokst
Everyone was thrown together
klaska mamook okoke huloima chee illahie.
to make this strange new country.

—from "Rain Language" by Terry Glavin,
in Charles Lillard's
A Voice Within Us: The Story of Chinook

CONTENTS

INTRODUCTION

The 1900 strike of salmon fishermen on the Fraser River, which shut down British Columbia's second-largest export industry and ended with the imposition of martial law, has long been understood as a watershed moment in the province's industrial history. In reality it was much more. The events of 1900 occurred against the emergence of BC's modern political system, particularly its distinctive conservative, liberal and radical-left party lines. Wracked by corruption scandals in the rail and mining industries, many involving leading political figures, the legislature was unable to produce a stable administration from the ever-shifting alliances of its members, none of whom were elected on party tickets. For a few weeks and months, as turmoil in the legislature weakened the already minimal forces of law and order, the doors slowly closed on the province's past—and fateful questions about race and economic power were settled for the next half century.

Other strikes in the same era lasted longer, and many were more violent. Many involved racial conflict at least as much as economic or class struggles. None, however, drew such diverse groups—Indigenous, Nikkei,[1] white—into an uneasy, short-term but effective coalition, defying the common wisdom that organizing across racial lines was either impossible or unacceptable. All were battles of the many against the few, but no strike confronted so directly the small group of men who exercised near absolute economic and political control over the life of the province. No wonder, then, when all else failed, that the cannery owners—universally referred to as "the canners"—arranged for the mobilization of more than two hundred soldiers, without recourse to the legislature or Parliament, to end the dispute even as they yielded to some of the strikers' demands.

The fishermen were united by their determination to win a decent living and a measure of economic and social equality. They were divided by equally forceful social pressures. The First Nations chiefs were trying not to be displaced by others, particularly the Nikkei, from a fishery they held as their Aboriginal right. The Nikkei, fleeing poverty in their homeland and well aware they could face expulsion from Canada, were seeking equality and opportunity in a new country where they could put down roots. The "white" fishermen, who included every ethnicity and nationality in the Americas and Europe, were miners, loggers, longshoremen, sailors and labourers. Angered by privilege and comfortable with socialist theory, they combined a frontier, gold-rush sensibility with a deep resentment of the tiny clique of wealthy Vancouver industrialists who controlled the salmon industry.

By the end of the strike and in its sequel in 1901, it was clear that Indigenous fishers would not dislodge the Nikkei, that the

Nikkei would not get the vote and, fatally, that division along racial lines would haunt the province for generations. The strike showed that many subsequent developments—the continued marginalization of First Nations, the expulsion of the Nikkei in 1942, the eventual decline of the salmon fishery, the extraordinary concentration of corporate power at the centre of the province's political system—were not inevitable, nor what most who lived in the province would have preferred. In this respect, the strike tells a story of hope, underlining the reality that no particular direction in history is the only option, and that people can, at least to a degree, envision new directions and work to achieve them.

Three people more than any others were at the centre of events on the strikers' side. They were not friends and had probably never even met before that year. They had no coordinated plan, but each had a strategic objective in the confrontation that they all expected. The oldest was barely forty. Each of these men was the product of dislocation; each reflected the diverse and profound conflicts that were reshaping every part of the world. Each of these men was asked to be the voice of his community, selected to lead in a struggle that both the fishermen and the canners anticipated and planned for. And although each was well known, even famous at the time (and later individually honoured in distinctive ways), all three remain mysterious figures.

Frank Rogers, who became president of the BC Fishermen's Union, was a longshoreman perhaps of American or Scots origin but a Canadian citizen, a socialist and a magnetic speaker. When he was killed barely three years later by a CPR policeman's bullet, the funeral march in his honour was one of the largest the city had ever seen.

Yasushi Yamazaki, a native of Toyama and the son of a samurai, variously a US navy ensign, seal hunter and newspaperman, was picked by the Nikkei to lead Dantai, or the Japanese Fishermen's Benevolent Association (JFBA), because of his combative attitude. Short and stocky, quick with his fists, familiar with business and bookkeeping, Yamazaki was a controversial and divisive figure. He was fluent in English and probably in Chinook, the distinctive Pacific Coast trading language that combined elements of Indigenous languages, French and English. Yamazaki later emerged as one of the most important leaders in Vancouver's Nikkei community as editor of the *Tairiku Nippo*, the *Continental Times*. It was Yamazaki who would later mobilize Nikkei volunteers to fight among the Canadians at Vimy Ridge, confident that this sacrifice would win the Nikkei the franchise. But by the time he had raised funds for the Nikkei war memorial in Stanley Park, it was clear his quest had been futile.

George Kelly was a mixed-blood Tsimshian man of noble lineage born in the Puget Sound area but raised in Victoria and Port Simpson. A sometime soap factory employee and a trumpet player in Nelson's Cornet Band in Port Simpson, Kelly was often the chief who addressed the crowd on behalf of the Aboriginal fishermen at rallies and demonstrations in 1900. Within seven years of the strike, the elders in his home community of Lax Kw'alaams, or Port Simpson, bestowed the name Lige'ex upon him, representing one of the most important honours and responsibilities in the Tsimshian community. Despite his prominent role in the 1900 strike and the great honour bestowed on him later, Kelly remains a shadowy figure. He left no personal memoir, his contemporaries left no tributes to him, his descendants know little about him and the only surviving picture shows him covering his face with a mask.

In the thirty years since the canning industry had been established, the numbers of canneries and fishermen grew exponentially, particularly in the last four years of the nineteenth century. A major consolidation in 1891 had failed to slow the breakneck expansion of canning and fishing capacity, both on the Fraser and in the massive salmon traps built on the American side of the boundary. The run of 1900 would be a precursor to the fabled Big Year run of 1901, the fourth-year peak of the sockeye cycle that choked the Fraser with fish. The price paid to fishermen in 1900 would set a level for 1901. If it was too high, the canners thought, they could lose everything; if it was too low, the fishermen believed, they would starve. Something had to give—everyone knew it. Who would win and who would lose? The canners, the white fishermen, the Nikkei and the First Nations leaders all understood what was at stake.

All these forces came together in Steveston, British Columbia's "Salmonopolis," a clapboard and cedar-shake cannery boomtown at the mouth of the Fraser that blossomed into one of the province's largest cities for a few hectic months each summer. Effectively unorganized territory, under the lax supervision of a pair of local police officers and accessible only by steamer or stagecoach, Steveston was a ramshackle hive of bars, hotels, brothels, pool halls, bunkhouses and machine shops organized behind a dozen canneries.

Located on the site of an old Musqueam village, Steveston was a quiet place until the salmon ran. Then, the town burst at the seams, recreating the global economy in a microcosm, with all its diversity and hierarchy. In effect a huge factory, Steveston was a place of opportunity where legal authority was weak, the power structure was clear and there was money to be made, at least by the canners. Along the river, interspersed between the canneries, were the segregated quarters of the white cannery supervisors, the China houses for cannery crews, the bunkhouses for Indigenous and Nikkei workers, and smaller quarters for the smaller numbers of Sikhs often seen working in unloading crews.

The nature of the fishery, which saw thousands of fishermen working close together on the grounds, sharing the risks of shoal water, unpredictable winds and uncertain salmon prices, fostered both a sense of personal self-reliance and collective self-interest. Fishermen well understood the four-year cycle of the sockeye, with the Big Year producing returns so massive that canners could slash prices at will and even limit the catch purchased from each boat. There were at least thirty canneries along the Fraser and its North Arm, controlled by about twenty Vancouver businessmen. In turn, they were directed by Henry Bell-Irving, whose Anglo-British Columbia (ABC) Packing Company counted for the largest share of the annual salmon pack.

As in the mining industry, where miners blamed contracted Chinese miners for breaking strikes in the coal fields, efforts to force a more equal distribution of the wealth of the salmon had always foundered on the divisions among the fishermen themselves. White fishermen had been the first to break during a strike in 1893, when the First Nations fleet stubbornly refused to yield. Ever since, the growing fleet of Nikkei fishermen on the Fraser had deterred both whites and Indigenous fishers from confronting the canners.

By 1900, a rising tide of unionization in the province produced the formation of a new fishermen's union in New Westminster and Vancouver. The Nikkei, worried about the price of salmon and their future in this new country, organized their own association both to bargain with the canners and to offer basic community services. Angry about low prices and their steady displacement by the Nikkei, Aboriginal fishers tended to cast their lot with the white, unionized fishermen, but their interests were different. Price was important, but for the chiefs who travelled to the Fraser, their right to participate in the fishery was at stake, threatened by the Nikkei, who now outnumbered them. Despite these divergent goals, the fishermen united in 1900, even if only briefly, against the canners.

There are moments in history when old ways lose their meaning and new structures have yet to be imposed. Unexpected possibilities come to light. Society can move in new directions or fall back on old patterns, divisions and prejudices. Such a moment occurred in Steveston in 1900. If there was one place in the province where the stresses and strains of BC's breakneck economic expansion could produce a confrontation over money and power, it was here. By spring, both canners and fishermen were making plans for the battle they knew would come. The result was not what anyone expected. It revealed, if only for a moment, the potential for a very different future for British Columbia than what transpired. It revealed, as well, how difficult such a change in course can be, especially if those in the midst of those events fail to understand or grasp their opportunity.

CHAPTER 1

VANCOUVER

Thousands left their jobs in Vancouver on the afternoon of October 23, 1899, to watch the volunteers of the Sixth Regiment, Duke of Connaught's Own Rifles (DCOR), march off through icy rain to the Boer War. Only twelve days earlier, the Boers had invaded the British colony of South Africa, and Vancouver had been in a fever of war preparations ever since. It was taken for granted that British Columbians, at least of a certain background, would rally to the defence of a colonial outpost on the other side of the world. Although at least fifty of the Sixth Regiment's three hundred soldiers had volunteered for active duty, only twenty-eight had been accepted in this first contingent, seventeen from Vancouver and eleven from New Westminster.

During the previous day's preparations at the regiment's drill hall, the part-time soldiers had whiled away the hours with desultory marching drills, flirtations with "a surplus of girls," sittings for formal photographs and a lengthy fare-well service before a packed congregation at St. Andrew's Church on Burrard. Those soldiers remaining behind teased the volunteers that their last night in Vancouver was drawing near, "and how, of course, they would leave their bones in the land of the Boers and the other South African hyenas." But no one looking on the volunteers, seated in full uniform in the first two rows of pews at St. Andrew's, could suppress what a *Vancouver Daily World* reporter described as "an intense feeling of pride—proud that he or she was a British subject, subject of an empire upon whose domains the sun never sets."[2]

A hastily launched public appeal for funds to assist the volunteers with out-of-pocket expenses on the way to war quickly raised more than $1,100. Although most of the dona-tions were only a dollar or five dollars, about ten of the city's leading citizens contributed twenty-five dollars each. (The average worker earned about five dollars a day.) Financier and salmon canner Henry Bell-Irving was in this group, happy to support the defence of the Empire and thinking, perhaps, that he might himself require the regiment's services to suppress alien forces closer to home.[3] Francis Carter-Cotton, publisher of the Vancouver *News-Advertiser*, chipped in twenty-five dollars, as did the Oppenheimer brothers. David Oppenheimer, after all, had been the city's second mayor. The owners of the *Province*, not to be outdone, led the campaign with a $100 gift.

Preceded by a brass band, the Dukes marched from their drill hall on Beatty Street to Granville Street, where the side-walks were thronged with citizens anxious to experience "some of the ardour and fighting glory of the men who were going to South Africa determined to win." At the Canadian Pacific Railway station at the foot of Granville, the crowds jammed the long stairway to the tracks from Hastings Street and filled the ramp down to the harbour, where the rain had turned the road to mud and clouds pressed down on the trees across Coal Harbour on Deadman's Island. "Cheer after cheer rent the air as the men boarded the train," reported the *World*, "but when the national anthem was played, the crowd could not control themselves. They broke into one mighty voice, singing the anthem with great fervor." When "God Save the Queen" had ended, the battalion band played a final chorus of "The Girl I Left Behind Me" and the crowd threw hundreds of hats and umbrellas in the air. The train jerked, then started rolling east.

The DCOR volunteers represented only a part of the new society forming in British Columbia. They were overwhelmingly drawn from recent Canadian, British and American arrivals to Vancouver, all of whom had shown up well after the catastrophic 1886 fire that had reduced the city to ashes. Most were under the age of twenty-five, and few had been in Vancouver more than three years. Although the DCORs were the epitome of the young white manhood idealized by the city's businessmen, editorial writers and clergy, they were very much the minority in a frontier town that drew its population from everywhere on the globe and largely from outside the British Empire.[4]

In the years since the arrival of the CPR in 1888, the city had grown from a few hundred residents to more than twenty thousand. Where old-growth forest had stood just twenty years before, there was now a modern city with gas streetlamps, a rudimentary telephone system and streetcars. A sturdy brick business district, flanked by residential neighbourhoods, lined the Burrard Inlet harbourfront all the way from the smokestacks and green chains of Hastings Mill, near the original city centre, to the hotels, rooming houses and warehouses of Gastown and the CPR terminal at the foot of Burrard Street. At these piers and wharves, steamers from Yokohama and Canton unloaded silk, tea and less exotic cargos before embarking passengers and freight for the return trip. These Pacific trade routes had emerged more than a century prior from the sea otter trade linking First Nations harvesters on Vancouver Island with traders along the entire Pacific seaboard from California to Alaska, Kamchatka and eventually Japan.

The Vancouver wharves had become the hub of a maritime trading system supporting British Columbia's coastal communities, most of them still First Nations. These routes included scores of salmon canneries, logging camps and mining concessions dependent on CPR or Union steamships for passenger and freight connections to the wider world. Since European contact had begun a century before, the centre of the province's non-Aboriginal economic life had shifted first from New Westminster, on the Fraser, to Victoria at the entrance to the Strait of Georgia, now known as the Salish Sea. The railway had moved it once more to Vancouver, the growing and undisputed heart of the provincial economy, which now counted mining, the salmon fishery and forestry as its main engines.

Vancouver was expanding at an explosive rate to keep pace with the growth in trade, which was being accelerated even further by Klondike gold seekers arriving daily to ship out for Alaska and the Yukon. The neighbourhood around the DCOR drill hall, east of Granville next to Larwill Park, was filled with new homes for families of modest means whose upstairs windows overlooked the rail yards, factories and foundries of False Creek.

Along the ridge to the west of Granville was a growing residential district of expansive homes, some designed by architects and qualifying as mansions. They housed the city's growing middle and upper classes in well-appointed comfort, with stone fireplaces warming drawing rooms furnished with costly imported armchairs and exotic fabrics. From Granville and Georgia, where the CPR was raising a magnificent new hotel, it was a short walk to False Creek, where the railway's roundhouse, machine shops and rail yards formed the centre of the city's heavy industry with shipyards, gas plants and sawmills that pushed right up to the edges of Chinatown. The CPR literally held Vancouver in its grip, with major rail yards hemming the young city in on two sides.

A new arrival looking for a place to stay in Vancouver had many options. The well-heeled could always find a comfortable room in hotels near the CPR station, an impressive new brick building with mansard roofs and a large central arch leading to the concourse. From the station it was just a block to the retail district on Hastings, with its working man's hotels and bars built hard up against the railway tracks. Even cheaper beds could be found in the flophouses of Chinatown on Dupont Street, or in the rooming houses among the Italian and Jewish homes of Strathcona. Nikkei arrivals often settled in an emerging community right across the tracks from Ballantyne Pier, where they disembarked from steamers. Entire Indigenous families from the coast could often be found camped on available stretches of beach along the harbourfront, their canoes dragged up on the rocks.

The population of this Vancouver east of Granville was much larger than the share from which the Dukes drew their volunteers. It included several thousand Chinese, a smaller but growing Nikkei population, the Squamish Nation residents of Snauq at the entrance to False Creek, and thousands of others from every part of the world who worked in the city's booming construction, manufacturing, longshore and rail sectors.[5] For these people, who had fled conflict, poverty and dislocation in their birthplaces, the outbreak of the Boer War was no cause for celebration. Perhaps more so than other cities emerging at the turn of the twentieth century, Vancouver was something distinct and new, although the city's growth meant a profound loss for the Musqueam, the Squamish and the Tsleil-Waututh on whose territory the metropolis was growing. Poet A.M. Stephen, who arrived in the "sordid and beautiful" city at about this time, concluded his ode "Vancouver" with the words, "... the sound of a wave, breaking on the shores of the future."[6]

The men and women who joined in lusty choruses of "Soldiers of the Queen" to send the Dukes on their way shared a common understanding of British Columbia as a growing and prosperous outpost of the British Empire. They ascribed the staggering riches flowing from the province's natural resources to their own business acumen and innate superiority. Not so the thousands of Chinese residents who had come as virtual slave labour to build the railroad, or the Nikkei arriving at the rate of hundreds a month, fleeing poverty and dislocation in their homeland. Their only option was to work: none had the right to vote and provincial law strictly limited the jobs at which they could legally earn a living.

Vancouver, like British Columbia, was still feeling its way in the modern world. A colony until 1871, the province had so far been dominated by political leaders bent more on unfettered resource extraction than good government. The end of colonial status had ushered in an era of "representative democracy" in which elected officials saw all politics through the lens of economic expansion, particularly the accumulation of profit by the few thousand white male electors who effectively governed the rest.

Unlike the rest of Canada, where political parties had emerged at the provincial level with organized slates and comprehensive platforms, British Columbia still had no party lines. Voters selected from lists of nominally independent candidates, some loosely seen as "government," others as "opposition" and still others by whatever label they fancied. Once elected, individual members of the legislature could cross from government to opposition at will, and some did.

The boom times brought by the railroad had faltered in the face of a global recession in 1893. The city's economic life did not revive until the Klondike gold rush began in 1898. John Turner, a salmon canner and ship chandler, had served as finance minister since 1887 and rose to premier in 1895. His government of "special interests, of railway industrialists, coal barons, wholesalers and importers, and lumber and salmon-canning capitalists" eased the way for wholesale transfers of provincial land to railway speculators, real estate promoters and mine developers.[7]

A new political movement based on the growing strength of the labour movement had attempted to end "Turnerism" in the 1898 election but had fallen short. Charles A. Semlin, a Fraser Canyon rancher and hotel operator who had served both as a member of Parliament and the legislature, was elected premier but could not stabilize his cabinet. Despite the election of labour-backed Vancouver candidates like Francis Carter-Cotton, a newspaper publisher; Robert Macpherson, a pharmacist with Liberal roots; and Joseph Martin, also a Liberal and a firebrand orator recently arrived from dramatic political conflicts in Manitoba, the 1898 election produced a divided house that was unable to govern.

Like many of those arriving in the province, politicians often had personal pasts they preferred to leave vague. Carter-Cotton, son of a pawnbroker, had been born in 1843 in London. His murky early years included an education in the classics and possibly a tour of duty in the British diplomatic corps before he landed in Wyoming to become owner of a vast tract of land linked to the Union Pacific Railroad. When that venture collapsed, he escaped creditors in 1886 by locking them in his office while he jumped on a departing train for Denver, Colorado. After a brief disappearance, he re-emerged in Vancouver to purchase two struggling newspapers that he consolidated into the *News-Advertiser*. He exploited the profile that the newspaper brought him to win a seat on city council and then the legislature, where he had served as an MLA since 1890. Once in office, Carter-Cotton was a voice for the working man, the scourge of "monopolists," and a reliable opponent of speculators and grafters.[8]

Carter-Cotton's unsteady ally and frequent opponent in the legislature was Fighting Joe Martin, then forty-six, a quarrelsome but charismatic lawyer who arrived in Vancouver in 1897 as legal counsel for the CPR. His turbulent Manitoba career had focused on attacking the privileges of the CPR, a contradiction his detractors could not resolve. His arrival prompted a *Province* editorial that begged Manitobans to keep Martin and send a blizzard in his stead. Martin ignored the naysayers and secured a Vancouver seat in the legislature in the election of 1898.[9]

The 1898 vote was so hotly contested that no one could be sure what had happened when it was over. Only sixteen members of the thirty-eight-member legislature had previous electoral experience; six incumbents were defeated. Twenty-nine ridings saw petitions seeking to challenge the outcome and the election of two members in the Cassiar region had been deferred. Matters were complicated by the manoeuvres of Lieutenant Governor Thomas McInnes, who was widely believed to be exercising his considerable powers to ensure his own private interests were protected. Determined to drive Turner out of office, McInnes went so far as to call on Robert Beaven to form a government, even though Beaven had not been able to get elected in 1894 or 1898.

When Beaven gave up after just four days, McInnes then prevailed on Semlin to lead the province. Semlin had little choice but to bring veterans like Carter-Cotton and Martin onto his front bench. The other members of Semlin's team reflected the new ascendancy of labour voters: Slocan metal miners had elected progressive R.F. Green; Nanaimo coal miners voted in Ralph Smith, their long-time union leader; Martin, Carter-Cotton and McPherson drew heavily on Vancouver union voters. The result was a new legislature that moved sharply to the left, purging Turnerite officials, banning Chinese labour underground and imposing an eight-hour day in metal mining. This last innovation, the "foolish eight-hour day," as Bell-Irving termed it, was the only signal the Vancouver establishment needed to know that this new government was headed in the wrong direction, to the degree it had one.

Bitter conflict between Carter-Cotton and Martin for ascendancy in the legislature left Semlin's administration adrift. Martin, appointed attorney general in Semlin's cabinet, inflamed relations by disclosing to the legislature Carter-Cotton's Colorado jail term for fraud. And he sealed his fate with Semlin by his performance at an infamous banquet in Rossland where he addressed a gathering of heckling mine owners as "white-shirted hobos," threatened to cancel construction of a new courthouse, and vowed, "I will get even with this crowd before I am done with you, you can depend on that." The evening ended in an unseemly fracas in the hotel lobby in which a heckler slapped Martin in the face and the attorney general scuffled with the mayor and a guest of honour.

On July 1, 1899, Semlin asked Martin to resign from cabinet in the wake of controversies over his private business activities and the Rossland fiasco. But Semlin himself was asked to resign a few months later when he sought to cobble together a new administration that included the hated Turner. McInnes dismissed Semlin's crowd and invited Martin to form government. This united the legislature—against Martin. For months, the capital was the focus of frantic scheming and chaotic confrontations. There was, fundamentally, no government in Victoria.[10]

For the most part, the absence of government suited Vancouver business interests, despite the worrisome pro-labour tilt of the Semlin gang. The canners and their financiers, whose industry was regulated far away by Ottawa, if at all, were not distracted by the provincial political chaos. The 1899 harvest proved unexpectedly large. The run in 1900, while not expected to be as bountiful as the following Big Year, would set the benchmark price for 1901. Bell-Irving, whose ABC Packing Co. canned the lion's share of the Fraser salmon pack, had been making plans for more than a year to maximize the 1901 return for his companies and the other canners who constituted an effective combine on the Fraser.

The son of a Glasgow merchant, Henry Ogle Bell-Irving trained as an engineer and emigrated to Canada in 1881 to work as a surveyor on the CPR. By 1886, he and his brother Dr. Duncan Bell-Irving had decided to settle in Granville, the Burrard Inlet community soon to become Vancouver. The two brothers lived in side-by-side houses on Alexander Street in the days after the fire, but Henry quickly traded up to a larger home on Seaton Street (now West Pender) and finally to The Strands, a sprawling, three-storey timbered mansion in the West End where stuffed stags' heads hung above chintz-covered furniture imported from England. Henry Bell-Irving quickly built up new businesses in real estate and the import-export trade and won election as a city alderman. His wife, Marie Ysabel del Carmen Beattie, was the daughter of a major sugar plantation owner in Santiago, Cuba, while a cousin was an executive at Jardine, Matheson and Co., the tea merchants that dominated much of British trade with China.[11]

Bell-Irving was able to mobilize all these connections in 1889 when he was approached to find cargo for the clipper ship *Titania*, about to return empty to the United Kingdom after delivering a load of steel rails to Vancouver. He filled the *Titania*'s hold with canned salmon. The resulting profits convinced him that here was a path to fortune. With the assistance of family connections in the United Kingdom, he quickly secured capital in 1890 to purchase options on several canneries to form Anglo-British Columbia Packing Co., vaulting him in a single move to the leadership of the largest salmon canning company in the province. By April of 1891, ABC had acquired seven more Fraser canneries and two on the Skeena, assuring Bell-Irving control of about 25 percent of the provincial pack and as much as 70 percent of the Fraser sockeye catch. In 1896, he revolutionized the industry a second time with the creation of the Automatic Can Company, a company that mechanized the manufacture of salmon cans that until then had been hand-built by Chinese labourers.

Energetic, entrepreneurial, rich, strategic, Bell-Irving had no peers in the leadership of the fishing industry. His own BC-based firm became the Canadian agent for ABC, which was registered in the UK, giving him a share of the profits of every aspect of the company's operations. As canner

Henry Doyle noted, the cannery agents "made a profit on what supplies they furnished to canners; on transportation charges on the ships they chartered; and they were paid a net 2½ percent brokerage fee of what the pack sold for if sent abroad." Bell-Irving kept all these revenues for himself. To grow profits further, he needed to cut the cost of salmon and increase the price paid in wholesale markets, so he set out to do both.[12]

Bell-Irving did everything he could to limit or eliminate what he considered the wasteful competition that resulted from a proliferation of new canneries on the Fraser, each with profit-hungry owners bidding against one another to secure salmon. He lobbied Ottawa tirelessly to limit investment in boats and canneries. His attempts to control the fishing sector through cannery ownership of gillnet licences had been defeated by the fishermen's political power in New Westminster and Vancouver. But Bell-Irving had alternatives. The free import of sockeye captured in massive traps on the American side of the line provided one solution to the growing organization of fishermen. The arrival of larger and larger numbers of Nikkei fishermen provided another: a group of gillnetters whose jobs depended on the canners' provision of licences or rental boats.

Bell-Irving thought he had decisively broken the fishermen's union in 1893. In the years after that strike, the canners shifted as much of the financial risk as possible to the fishermen themselves, first switching from a daily wage to a price per fish and then lobbying hard for the allocation of fixed numbers of boats to each cannery. They preferred these cannery fleets to be crewed by Indigenous or Nikkei fishers, whose services could be secured through contractors who handled all the complexities of housing, pay distribution and food in return for a share of the gross. In this respect, the

Nikkei fishers offered a unique advantage: unlike Indigenous fishers, they lacked the leverage First Nations leaders exercised through their control of a large share of the cannery workforce, which was built on the labour of Indigenous women. Nor were the Nikkei free to leave for their home village, as First Nations fishers and shoreworkers could, if they became dissatisfied with pay or conditions.

Bell-Irving made no secret of his preference for an open market in labour, in which Chinese and Nikkei workers could be imported as required to dampen the militancy of the existing workforce. With typical candour, he declared that the Chinese were "less trouble and less expense than whites. They are content with rough accommodation at the canneries ... I look upon them as steam engines or any other machine, the introduction of which deprives men of some particular employment but in the long run, it enormously increases employment." Of course, he added, with an eye to political realities, Chinese workers would not be required if "satisfactory white labour were obtainable."[13]

Yet Bell-Irving was unable to suppress white fishermen's discontent indefinitely. By 1896, fishermen were meeting at the Steveston Opera House to lobby Ottawa for a prohibition on fishing by anyone other than provincial voters, and a ban on the import of trap fish. At the very least, fishermen wanted stringent enforcement of the "naturalization" papers readily available to Nikkei and American fishermen, who were required to demonstrate residency to obtain a licence.

In 1898, when fishermen's lobbying efforts produced new federal regulations, including a sharp reduction in cannery licences, Bell-Irving succeeded in creating the BC Salmon Canners' Association with the aim of forcing Ottawa to retreat. By August, however, it was clear he would be only partly successful. The canners required cannery or "attached" licences because they could compel "attached" fishermen to deliver to their canneries, whereas independent fishermen could sell to whomever they pleased. A joint committee of canners and fishermen, created by Liberal members of Parliament to find a compromise, broke down when fishermen insisted the canners retain access to only ten boat licences each at a time when several thousand gillnetters were setting their nets at every weekly opening. Such a low number would dramatically strengthen the fishermen's bargaining power. It was a sign of the labour movement's growing strength that Joseph Henry Watson, a committed Liberal and president of the Vancouver Trades and Labour Council, was a full member of that committee. Bell-Irving succeeded in restoring some of the cannery licences, but the gains won by the fishermen underlined their growing political clout—at least of those who had a vote.

Patriarch of a growing family and a corporate fortune at the age of only forty-four, Bell-Irving moved once more to expand his combine, creating the Fraser River Canners' Association (FRCA) to manage the fishery for the 1900 season. Only three of the river canners declined to join. By June, preparations for the upcoming confrontation with the fishermen were well advanced. The association had cultivated close relations with the Japanese consulate. At their meeting on June 26, Bell-Irving, Thomas Ladner and others had agreed to hire three special police at between $75 and $100 a month each and to ask Attorney General David Eberts for the authority to have their men sworn in as special constables.

At the same meeting, they fixed the maximum price they would pay for salmon at twenty cents. Their opening position would be five cents less. When it came to the salmon industry, Bell-Irving pretty much called the shots. "He thought he was the boss of everything," a contemporary recalled, and he wasn't far wrong. The fishermen, however, had plans of their own.[14]

CHAPTER 2

NELSON'S CORNET BAND

In early June 1900, Ned DeBeck stood on the dock of Steveston's Scottish Canadian Cannery, scanning the Fraser River's main channel for the Indigenous fishermen and cannery workers expected to arrive at any moment from the north. Finally, he spotted sails out at Sand Heads light, the fifty-foot hexagonal wooden lighthouse on stilts that sat where the Fraser's silt-laden flow merged with the blue water of the Strait of Georgia. "Here they came on a flood tide," he wrote later, "bowling along ahead of a westerly wind, great canoes fifty feet and over, spread to an eight-foot beam, each with four sails wing on wing. Some came all the way from the Skeena, but more were Kwakiutl."

There were twenty-four canoes in the flotilla, half at least twelve metres long, twelve even larger, "packed with men, women and children." Some of the canoes continued upstream, but a dozen turned to land at the cannery, and "in the last few hundred yards, sails were lowered and they started singing Indian songs until they got to five or six yards from the wharf. With a final shout, a sudden silence for about a minute. Then the biggest chief stood up and, with speaking staff in hand, made a short speech. A sudden stop, a barked order and then all hell broke loose, every paddle clawing water to sidle the canoe up to the wharf."

The children poured ashore first, desperate to stretch after a ride that had brought them from Cape Mudge, at the south end of Johnstone Strait, to the Sand Heads—a distance of 210 kilometres—in just twenty-four hours. Beds, bedding and tents were quickly passed ashore, fires were lit and within hours the camp was established "as though it had existed for months, with fires burning and dogs barking and fowls cackling and [an] ancient fish-like smell asserting its supremacy."[15]

The Scottish Canadian Cannery stood at Steveston's Garry Point, the former site of a Musqueam village that had constantly been undermined by the Fraser's shifting sands. The point itself, a sandspit pointing seaward where the Fraser emptied through broad sandbanks into the Strait of Georgia, was dominated for many years by a single tall pine, the centre point of a vast amphitheatre bounded by the mountains to the south, north and east, and the Strait on the west. From his vantage point on the dock, DeBeck could see the Gulf Islands and Vancouver Island's Mount Arrowsmith to the west, and on a sunny day, the distant peaks of the Olympic Peninsula running out to the Pacific. To the southeast, Mount Baker's volcanic summit rose far above its neighbours and to the east, DeBeck could pick out Cheam Peak and Mount Slesse at the end of the Fraser Valley, where the Fraser met the mountains and turned north.

Steveston stood midway between the province's three major cities but was isolated from all of them by water. Victoria was a half-day cruise to the west and New Westminster was several hours upstream. Vancouver could be reached only by a similar steamer trip north or by a dusty, day-long stagecoach-and-ferry trip over land, across the Fraser and through miles of old-growth forest south of the city. Steveston was defined by the Fraser, which reached the Strait of Georgia at Sand Heads more than ten kilometres seaward of DeBeck's vantage point.

The Musqueam had harvested sea lions, seals, salmon, oolichans and sturgeon in the Fraser, as well as the abundant berries that grew in the delta's fertile soil.[16] The summer migration of coastal Indigenous communities to the Fraser long predated the arrival of the salmon canneries. The fur traders who built Fort Langley in 1827 were startled in August of that year when scores of canoes passed by, headed upstream to fish in the lower Fraser Canyon, where Sto:lo chiefs controlled key fishing spots. In subsequent years, hundreds of Indigenous men and their families travelled down the Inside Passage annually to Victoria for summer trading, many then carrying on to Puget Sound to work in the sawmill industry, or to Sto:lo territory around what is now Chilliwack for fishing. The annual cycle often ended in the hop fields that were later planted in the Fraser Valley, where First Nations from around the province camped and celebrated the end of the work season with dances and feasts.[17]

Fort Langley itself relied on Sto:lo fishers to harvest salmon, and the Sto:lo women who butchered the fish, for what became an important salt salmon trade with Hawaii. When Alexander Ewen, a veteran of Scotland's salmon fishery, converted his New Westminster salmon saltery to canning in 1871, he required Indigenous fishers and cannery workers to complete his pack, a total of three hundred cases for export to the United Kingdom. From that small start, the industry grew year after year, with cannery after cannery built along the Fraser's banks from New Westminster to Garry Point.[18]

By 1900, Steveston was a farming community for most of the year, sheltered behind modest dykes at the edge of the Fraser's sprawling and shifting delta, and home to a few hundred year-round residents including a growing community of Nikkei. But the arrival of the salmon runs made this sleepy village the province's fourth-largest city for a hectic eight-week period—a complex factory dedicated to landing and canning millions of sockeye. Other BC towns may have been built around a mine, smaller communities around a farming district or a sawmill, but Steveston required thousands of workers each summer for assembly-line mass production.

Steveston's main streets were rough-sawn boardwalks. Its largest buildings were two storeys high, with the exception of the broad-roofed canneries, their net lofts and their warehouses. Civic government consisted of a rudimentary village council for Richmond, the scattered farming community that lay on Lulu Island, bounded by the Fraser's main stem on the south and the North Arm on the Vancouver side. Legal authority rested with a handful of police officers who focused on maintaining peace in the town's bars and brothels, and a tiny group of fisheries overseers in rowboats, sometimes backed up by a steam tug.

Housing was organized strictly along racial lines: Japanese bunkhouses for the Nikkei; "China houses" for the cannery crews; "Indian houses" for the Indigenous people unable or unwilling to sleep on the beach (in reality these "houses" were more like barracks). Apart from the Steveston Opera House, which seated up to four hundred, and a few establishments like the newly built Sockeye Hotel, the canneries dominated the riverfront with their long, high-pitched roofs, brick chimneys and L-shaped wharves, built to accommodate the square-riggers that arrived every fall to ship the pack to England and Australia.

Once the families landing at Scottish Canadian had settled in, there was much to do. Most of them had been contracted through a middleman, often a chief himself, who advanced food, clothing and cash in return for a season-long commitment. A good run and a higher fish price would mean much greater take-home pay, but poor runs and low prices could spell disaster. These arrangements would need finalizing, but in 1900 even more important discussions were underway. Negotiations among the canners, the BC Fishermen's Union and the Nikkei over the price of salmon had already begun. The First Nations fishers, who had seen their own attempted strike in 1899 broken by the Nikkei, were anxious to engage.

The elegant dugout canoes used to set the first Fraser gillnets had been replaced over the years by stout planked skiffs, but First Nations fishermen still made up a large share of the fleet. For nearly a generation, Indigenous fishers dominated the commercial harvest. That dominance, however, was fading. Year after year, First Nations fishers saw their opportunities to gillnet being usurped by newcomers, particularly the Nikkei then arriving in the Lower Mainland. Only ten licences were fished by Nikkei in 1888, but by 1893 there were 235. First Nations fishers had numbered 615 in 1887— about 60 percent of the total fleet—then saw their number decline to about 300 before rebounding to 558 in 1893, barely half of that year's fleet. It was clear throughout the 1890s that the Nikkei fleet would continue to grow, at the expense of Indigenous gillnetters and their families. There was no chance that politically powerful white fishermen would see their numbers decline. Nor did First Nations fishers have access to the new category of individual independent licences then being issued to white and even some Nikkei fishers.

Worse, the 1890s had seen coast-wide attempts to limit First Nations fisheries on their own territories. Nearly twenty years earlier, Ottawa had begun restricting Indigenous fisheries to personal consumption and local trade. This apparent confirmation of Indigenous fishing rights had been turned into its opposite: a limit on the amount of fish that First Nations could harvest. Sale of "food fish" was prohibited, shutting down the long-standing commerce in salmon and other fish products. This change meant little in the years after 1875, when the new regulations came into effect, because they were largely unenforceable. But when canners used access to upriver fisheries to evade closed times in the lower Fraser, federal fisheries overseers intervened to provide some minimum level of conservation close to the spawning grounds. The burden of these closures fell on Indigenous fisheries.

First Nations fishing rights, including ownership of specific fishing locations, were ignored and the sale of First Nations catches was suppressed. Yet when the gillnet licences attached to canneries were reduced, starting in 1893, that reduction also fell most heavily on First Nations fishers, who lost hundreds of jobs. The only reason some remained, according to the testimony of pioneer canner Alexander Ewen to a fisheries inquiry in 1891, was that it was "impossible to put up a large quantity of fish ... unless you have Indian labour."[19]

Indigenous fishers arriving in Steveston in 1900 were determined to achieve two gains: a minimum price of twenty-five cents and limitation, if not elimination, of Nikkei fishers, who now numbered 1,600 to the First Nations' 550.

Without some alliance with white fishermen, expected to number about a thousand, neither goal seemed achievable. Time was running out to protect their place in the Fraser fishery; they hoped the union could offer a way forward.

About the same time DeBeck watched the canoes land at Steveston, a further eight hundred Indigenous men, women and children disembarked from a CPR coastal steamer at the Evans, Coleman and Evans dock on the Vancouver waterfront. The new arrivals had travelled from Tsimshian and Nisga'a communities, but most were from Port Simpson, or Lax Kw'alaams. They had travelled the Inside Passage in the cheapest accommodation, often sleeping amid stacks of baggage, much of it on deck. Carefully stowed, however, were the boxed instruments and ceremonial uniforms of Nelson's Cornet Band, the Port Simpson brass band that formed one of the most important institutions of community life.

The Port Simpson people quickly moved ashore and set up camp on empty land between the railway tracks and Alexander Street just a few blocks east of the emerging Nikkei community on Powell Street. They would remain for a few weeks, enjoying the lights of the big city before moving to the canneries in Steveston. In spite of a widespread search, two Port Simpson men who headed straight to the bars were not seen again for thirty-six hours. Others immediately headed for the home of Reverend A.E. Green, the Methodist missionary who had lived for many years in Port Simpson, to plan their participation in the upcoming Dominion Day parade. The Port Simpson float would be decked in bunting and the march would feature Nelson's Cornet Band in distinctive blankets, painted with traditional designs, that had been produced for the occasion.[20]

Thousands thronged Vancouver's downtown for the July 2 parade route, which began at city hall on Westminster

Avenue, now Main Street, and proceeded through the crowds along Hastings Street. The Port Simpson band was one of three providing music, while the actors of the Alhambra Theatre entertained with a blackface minstrel show. Float after float rolled down Hastings Street, including an ambitious entry by the Sons of the British Empire drawn by four horses and preceded by a stout bulldog clenching two Union Jacks in its teeth, which received waves of applause. The float was ringed with the national symbols of the Empire, with England, Scotland and Ireland flanked by Canada, Australia "and the other colonies." Two members of the Duke of Connaught's Own Rifles, whose colleagues were still serving against the Boers in South Africa, stood rigidly at attention alongside a soldier in khaki. Oddly, a Klondike miner dressed as a Highlander played the pipes. "Mrs. Elliot represented the Goddess of Liberty," the *Vancouver Daily World* reported.

Not far behind the remarkable Pioneer Laundry float, which included an entire working laundry, came the Port Simpson band "in their full war paint and Rocky Mountain winter plumage and attire." The band not only played "very sweetly," the *World* declared, but "came in very properly as representatives of the bogies in the minds of unruly children who had come down to see the parade."

Pictures of the band taken a year later, as they prepared for a command performance before His Royal Highness, the Duke of Cornwall, show about twenty-five members in coordinated blankets decorated in distinctive North Coast designs, many wearing Tsimshian hats and elaborate cedar collars, others brandishing bows and arrows. Their grave but self-confident demeanour suggests they saw themselves as much more than the usual church brass band. They were a distinctively Tsimshian ensemble, proud of their widely acknowledged musicianship and their Aboriginal heritage.

Only one of the men is wearing a mask. He was George Kelly, spokesman for First Nations during the 1900 Fraser River strike. Was he hiding? Or seeking attention? Either is possible.[21]

If Steveston was the summer border town of BC's coastal communities, a lawless frontier town of boardwalks, bars and brothels, Port Simpson was its northern counterpart, a trading centre close to the mouth of the Skeena facing out onto Dixon Entrance and the open Pacific. The location had been selected by the Hudson's Bay Company in 1834, in consultation with Tsimshian chiefs, for a trading post and fort. The arrangement proved advantageous for both sides, generating a steady flow of sea otter and beaver pelts to HBC and allowing Tsimshian chiefs to consolidate their control over existing trade routes to the Interior.

Foremost among these chiefs was Lige'ex, or Legaic, whose control over trade extended even to regulation of the price of furs. The first Lige'ex was the son of a Tsimshian Eagle woman from Metlakatla and a Bella Bella chief. It was his successor and nephew, the second Lige'ex, who did the most to extend and consolidate control of the inland trade routes, marrying his daughter to the HBC's Dr. John Kennedy sometime after the new fort was established. Lige'ex was one of the few Indigenous people granted inoculation against the recurrent scourge of smallpox, a privilege the traders usually kept to themselves. The third Lige'ex was leading the community, now largely living at Port Simpson, when missionary William Duncan arrived late in 1857.[22]

The existence of such a large permanent population around the fort—in 1857 it was estimated at twenty-three hundred—made Port Simpson a desirable target for missionaries. Nine distinct tribes of the Tsimshian peoples moved to Lax Kw'alaams (Port Simpson) during the nineteenth century, their longhouses crowding around the bastions and stockade of the fort, their canoes and totems lining the beach. One of the first missionaries to dedicate his efforts to the Tsimshian was William Duncan, an Anglican lay preacher from Yorkshire dispatched by the Church Mission Society. He prepared the ground carefully, learning Tsimshian from elder Arthur Wellington Clah, who could both read and write English. Duncan opened a school in 1858 and soon made inroads among the Tsimshian, eventually vying with Lige'ex for influence over the community.

The chaotic environment around the fort, where alcohol was readily available, was not conducive to a quiet, worshipful life. In 1862, Duncan decided to lead his converts to Metlakatla to create a new, Christian community. Their departure, just two weeks before a smallpox epidemic originating in Victoria carried off hundreds of Tsimshian in Port Simpson, seemed to indicate that Duncan enjoyed divine protection. Duncan combined his religious leadership with a determination to integrate the Tsimshian into the wage economy, driving them to build a sawmill, install modern lighting and create a village of clapboard homes at Metlakatla complete with boardwalk streets, a store, warehouses and eventually an imposing wooden church in the English style.

By the mid-1870s, Duncan had organized the men and women of Metlakatla into ten companies "for mutual assistance, to keep each member of our community under observation (surveillance) and to give opportunities to the majority of our men to be useful to the commonwealth." The success of Metlakatla brought Duncan international acclaim as well as financial contributions. A decisive moment in the history of Metlakatla occurred when Lige'ex himself (there is confusion about how many held this title, but at least three did in the nineteenth century) moved to Duncan's new utopia. This conversion was hailed by Duncan as a repudiation of the Tsimshian life by a man at the peak of power and prestige, but Lige'ex's biographer, Michael Robinson, suggests that Lige'ex was seeking to extend his influence, not eliminate it. By converting to Anglicanism, he sought to "gain the spiritual power of the whites to complement the powers he already controlled."[23]

Duncan's autocratic style, and his unique combination of religious and economic power, soon brought him into conflict with Church of England clergy in Victoria and even in London. To escape their oversight, Duncan eventually led an exodus from Metlakatla as well, moving his flock in 1887 to New Metlakatla, in Alaska, where the entire process began anew. (This final move was too much for Lige'ex, who returned to Port Simpson.) By 1900, Edward Marsden, the son of Duncan's first convert and himself a Presbyterian minister, began to challenge Duncan's rule and New Metlakatla became as consumed in division and acrimony as its predecessor had been.

In stark contrast to Duncan's bleak crusade was the benign dictatorship of Robert Cunningham, an Irishman who had moved to Port Simpson to assist Duncan but left the town and religious life in 1870, eventually founding his own new community at Port Essington, where the Ecstall River flows into the mouth of the Skeena from the south. This cannery town, called Spaksuut in the Tsimshian language, was a string of homes, a store, a cold storage and a hotel, all on pilings and linked by boardwalks. It had a decidedly secular tone despite the presence of two churches. It was wholly owned by Cunningham. The man who had cut his ties to Duncan amid allegations of rum-running now owned a cannery, the townsite and almost everything else of value.

During salmon season, Port Essington was the north's party place, especially on Saturday nights, when the action centred on a boardwalk grandly named Dufferin Street:

> [It was] a seething mass of humanity, with represen-
> tatives of every race, and the vast majority of them in
> some degree of intoxication. The married women of
> the town very wisely stayed at home on Saturday night
> for the two Provincial constables were totally inad-
> equate to maintain order; and brawling frequently
> halted the stream of people as they eddied around a
> struggling group. In fact, the constables were often
> as bad as their charges and at one time were directly
> interested in the operation of the numerous gambling
> dens which were mulcting the careless fishermen ...
> Stores and restaurants stood open all evening and
> threw their shafts of light onto darkened streets.

Off the back lanes leading to the forest were shacks used by cannery workers and "others whose profession is the oldest known to man."[24]

The HBC had dealt Lige'ex and his successors a heavy blow with the development of sternwheeler service to Hazelton in the 1890s, undermining the Tsimshian monopoly on freight service to the headwaters of the Skeena. In 1900, Robert Cunningham's new sternwheeler *Hazelton* made the trip to the Skeena's headwaters in just forty hours. The dramatic expansion of the industrial economy, which had largely replaced the fur trade by mid-century, was trans-forming Tsimshian society but not destroying it. Tsimshian, Haida, Nisga'a and other First Nations communities in the north began making the thousand-kilometre canoe journey to Victoria and Puget Sound to trade and find work.

The Tsimshian, outstanding mariners and fishers, were at home on the sea. Many participated in the sea otter harvest and the fur seal fishery, which pursued the seals on their Pacific migration right to their rookeries in the Aleutians. Alfred Dudoward (Chief Sgagweet) owned the schooner *Georgia* and traded for many years between Port Simpson and Victoria. Many found work in the canneries, both on the Skeena and the Fraser, as well as in the annual migrations that took extended families first to the canneries, then perhaps to Puget Sound's sawmills and onto the Fraser Valley's hop farms before the journey home for the winter.

Despite the expansion of the steamboat trade, Port Simpson and Port Essington still provided the connections between the inland and upriver villages of the Tsimshian First Nations. Port Simpson and its permanent population of about eight hundred remained the hub of Tsimshian life in 1900. Its churches, schools and trade facilities were "the centre of north coast commerce, politics and culture." Methodist missionary Thomas Crosby arrived in Port Simpson in 1873, filling the void left by Duncan. The two missionaries, in the words of a leading history of the Tsimshian peoples, "not only represented Christian churches, but ... embodied the goals of the British Empire, which was to bring British values, beliefs and culture to the indigenous peoples of the world ... So it was that the missionaries came not only with the desire to spread the gospel, but to replace Ts'mysen culture with their own."[25]

Despite the dramatic changes of the previous twenty-five years—the end of the fur trade, the devastation of smallpox, the divisions triggered by the missionaries, the legal attacks on the potlatch and the imposition of the Indian Act— the Tsimshian remained resolute in their determination to persist and prosper on their land. In 1885, Duncan and three Tsimshian chiefs met with Prime Minister Sir John A. Macdonald to discuss the land question and the conflicts created by the Church Missionary Society's claim of two acres in Metlakatla. That winter, a delegation of chiefs made a difficult winter journey to Victoria to meet Premier William Smithe to seek a treaty, a demand he considered "simply misguided."[26]

It was not easy. The heavy losses caused by the smallpox epidemics caused continuing turmoil in Tsimshian society, wiping out entire families and cutting down scores of important leaders. Finding appropriate replacements was often difficult. When Paul Legaic (the last Lige'ex male) died in 1894, his sister Martha was still in her teens when she was appointed as the new official name holder.

By 1900, the walls of the HBC fort had been torn down and most of the Port Simpson residents, heeding the demands of the missionaries, had disposed of their regalia and moved out of their longhouses into frame homes. A long pier led from the dock to the HBC shops behind the town's beach and a second causeway linked the main village to Rose Island, where many of the residents had their homes. The few remaining longhouses fell into ruin and the new homes, arranged in straight rows overlooked by a large church, were the simple single-family houses familiar from countless company towns. Regular steamer service connected Port Simpson to Vancouver, and the village boasted its own boatyard, sawmill and machine shop. For the small white community—the HBC manager, the postmaster, a few shop owners, the clergy, the teachers and their wives—life was a close approximation of genteel Victorian society, highlighted by weekend tea parties in well-appointed drawing rooms with seafood and venison substituted for traditional English fare.

For the Tsimshian, private life had evolved into a distinctive new culture that merged longstanding Tsimshian family and political practices with the requirements of Christian missionary teaching. The most visible of these new institutions were the community's brass bands, run entirely by the Tsimshian, which combined the hierarchy and love of music in Tsimshian society with the paramilitary regalia of a church brass band. Public celebrations in Port Simpson were dominated by the Port Simpson Brass Band, which could often be heard performing in the community band shell when not leading a wedding or funeral procession. Based on its many competitive awards and its presence at ceremonial events of provincial significance, including performances before British royalty, the Port Simpson band, also called Nelson's Cornet Band, was the best in British Columbia.

Duncan considered the creation of a church band a key element of his pastoral program. In Port Simpson, the brass band "was an amazement to visitors," who were told how Tsimshian children "learned to read difficult classical music before they learned to read more than basic English." Helen Meilleur, whose father operated the HBC store in the early years of the twentieth century, recalled hearing the sounds of the band's performance of Tchaikovsky's "Waltz of the Flowers," played with "spirit and precision," drifting through the open windows of her bedroom on summer afternoons. "Their ancestral music led them into the works of Haydn and Mozart as naturally as a river falls into the sea," Meilleur recalled. "It was a marching band in red and gold, much gold."

On her walks through town, Meilleur could hear members of the sixty-man fire brigade conducting their band rehearsal in the fire hall while members of the Rifle Company, a volunteer militia, practised their tunes across the street. By 1896, there also were at least three denominational bands—Anglican, Methodist and Salvation Army—all vying for adherents on the streets of Port Simpson.[27] Missionaries also remarked on how quickly the Tsimshian took up religious choral singing, easily mastering four-part harmonies.

The Port Simpson bands, like those of many northern First Nations communities, were much more than a community pastime. They were a means by which "Aboriginal social, political and cultural interests were served and advanced through musical performance." They constituted the persistence of "older cultural identities and practices" in a new form that both responded to colonial culture and subverted it. As the coverage of their performance in Vancouver's Dominion Day Parade in 1900 makes clear, the Nelson's Cornet Band of Port Simpson made an impact. By being as good as any brass band anywhere, the men of Nelson's Cornet Band challenged watchers to see them as equals.

George Kelly played trumpet in that band.[28] Then about forty, Kelly lived in two worlds. He had experienced the full range of BC society, from the elite mansions of post-colonial Victoria to the frame houses of Port Simpson, spending at least some of his adult years in each community. The Victoria city directory lists a George Kelly who worked as a soap factory hand in that city in 1893; if it was the same George Kelly, factory labour was only part of his work experience. Kelly had come to Vancouver and Steveston to fish. When that was done, he would likely join the annual migration of First Nations workers from the salmon fishery to the hop fields of the Fraser Valley.[29] The son of a white father and Tsimshian mother, he was born in the Puget Sound logging town of Port Ludlow, Washington, where it was commonplace for workers—whether white or First Nations—to move from sawmilling to cannery work as the opportunity arose.[30]

Kelly likely knew little of his parents. His mother died when he was very young; her name and the name of his father are unknown. He was adopted by Elizabeth Diex, his mother's clan sister, then a Victoria domestic worker but also one of the leading matriarchs of the Tsimshian people, a noble woman of the Gitando clan. Born in a village near Port Simpson, she had fled to the HBC post to avoid marriage to a much older Tsimshian man, eventually marrying an HBC employee named Felix Dudoire (later Anglicized to Dudoward), with whom she bore a son, Alfred, in 1850. Alfred Dudoward became Chief Sgagweet, one of the most important Tsimshian leaders of his generation.[31]

During the 1860s and early 1870s, Diex worked in Victoria as a servant in the home of Judge Joseph Pemberton, a former Hudson's Bay Company surveyor who had laid out the Victoria townsite and many others. A surviving photo of her, likely taken during this period, shows a woman with a calm, confident, direct gaze. By the time the picture was taken, she had moved from a Tsimshian village to the HBC post and then to the heart of Victoria's colonial society.

Kelly may have been a visitor in Pemberton's household until his mother lost her job over allegations of theft, giving him a glimpse of elite Victoria life while he was still under the guardianship of one of the most important matriarchs in the Tsimshian community. In 1873, when Kelly was only about thirteen, Diex's life took another sharp turn when she converted to Methodism at a revival meeting in Victoria. The meeting was organized in a barroom converted to a place of worship and the meeting produced a wave of conversions, Diex foremost among them. This was certainly not her first encounter with Christianity or missionaries—her son Alfred and probably George Kelly had attended the boys' school in Port Simpson run by the Anglicans.

Those converted that night, especially Diex, begin spreading the Gospel themselves. Diex's first convert was her own son Alfred, then heading to Victoria by canoe to acquire rum, by some accounts, for an upcoming feast. Within months she had led the conversion of scores of other Indigenous residents in Victoria. Was Dudoward really travelling by canoe, not his schooner? Had he not converted much earlier? There is evidence to support both scenarios, but the tale was improved by the Methodists to great effect in flyers and sermons that circulated coastwide.[32]

Methodist missionary Thomas Crosby, who described Elizabeth Diex as "a woman of commanding appearance and of great force of character, who exerted a powerful influence over her people," prevailed on her to return to Port Simpson in 1874. She remained there at least ten years, returning to Victoria by 1887, when she married customs officer Robert Lawson, who himself had spent time in Port Simpson. As a result, George Kelly lived in both white and Tsimshian worlds. He was a voter, he emphasized in his speeches, meaning he did not have the Indian status that would deny him the vote.

Yet George Kelly remained Tsimshian because of his mother's heritage. To the Tsimshian, this was the decisive factor in their matrilineal society. Dudoward, son of Diex and the Quebecois HBC carpenter Dudoire, became Chief Sgagweet, owner of an imposing three-storey timbered Victorian home in Port Simpson with a large verandah and ample gingerbread. Dudoward's wife was Kate Holmes, daughter of another former HBC customs officer and a Tsimshian matriarch who became a domestic servant in Victoria as Diex had done.

When her mother died en route to Port Simpson to take up her title and rank, Holmes was installed as chief in her place but also preached Christianity in her community. When Dudoward and Holmes married in 1871, they combined power and influence from both Indigenous and Christian missionary currents of Tsimshian society. They moved as easily between Port Simpson and Victoria as a modern-day commuter might travel from Port Moody to Vancouver. No doubt, Kelly often travelled with them.[33]

Kelly was termed a chief in news reports. Whether or not he held that status in Tsimshian society, this title was indicative of the esteem he had achieved in the community. He was the adoptive son of a leading matriarch who maintained close ties with Crosby, one of the most influential Christian leaders on the north coast. He could read and write English, and spoke Tsimshian and Chinook. As a member of Port Simpson's most prestigious brass band, he was among the head men of the community, who held leading positions in the band as a matter of course. Other Tsimshian leaders had similar qualifications, including those who had met the premier and the prime minister to push for land rights. But First Nations chiefs had a direct message they wanted to deliver during the 1900 salmon fishery, and they apparently agreed that Kelly should deliver it. While other chiefs were mentioned in news reports in the weeks that followed, it was Kelly who spoke for Indigenous people at rallies and marches.[34]

By 1900, Tsimshian fishers had participated in many strikes, both on the Skeena and the Fraser, to secure better prices. When a sudden strike swept the Fraser in 1893 over licencing, fish prices and wage rates, the fleet divided sharply along race lines. The newly formed Fraser River Fishermen's Protective and Benevolent Association, the white fishermen's organization, demanded expulsion of the Nikkei fishermen then joining the fleet, controls on trap fishing and a ban on Americans fishing on Canada's side of the boundary. An appeal from Nikkei fishers to coordinate their efforts with the whites was spurned. When strike action began, Henry Bell-Irving successfully enlisted the assistance of the Japanese consul to recruit as many as four hundred Nikkei fishermen to break the strike, then raised wage rates for First Nations fishers.

Indian agents and police rushed to the Fraser in an effort to browbeat First Nations fishers into returning to work, without success. The Indian agent should do less to support the canners and more to support the fishers, said Chiefs Capilano George, Cranberry Jack and Charles Meshell, who complained their wages were so poor they needed to travel to jobs in four different cities to make ends meet. But the strike soon crumbled as white fishermen trickled back to work, weakly acknowledging that no Indigenous fishers "had volunteered to assist the canners until some white men had led the way."[35]

Prices rose as high as twenty-five cents a fish in subsequent years of low runs, but when sudden gluts overwhelmed the canners, they quickly slashed prices or limited the deliveries they would accept. Steady growth in the size of the fleet reduced individual average catches. First Nations gillnetters, earning flat daily rates, were unable to share in the windfalls or deliver extra when boat limits were imposed. In 1897, the next Big Year run, they announced they would strike for twenty-five cents a fish, a demand supported by Nikkei fishers but only grudgingly endorsed by the whites, who quickly went fishing when offered only ten cents. As the run built up in August 1897, the canneries were again flooded with fish. Prices fell as low as two cents apiece, and then boat limits imposed by canners cut the overall catch. As many as 100,000 fish a day were discarded.[36] Prices again soared in the low-run years of 1898 and 1899, when spot prices broke through twenty-five cents and rose as high as thirty cents. Clearly there was money to be won if the fishermen were tough enough to remain tied up.

The 1893 betrayal of the First Nations fleet by the white fishers remained a vivid memory for chiefs arriving on the Fraser in 1900. Even more threatening was the explosive growth of the Nikkei fleet, which now outnumbered First Nations boats. When union organization revived in the salmon industry in 1899, Port Simpson fishers were quick to form their own local of the BC Fishermen's Union. If the land claims movement was a strategic response to social, economic and cultural pressures, then unionization was a tactical one. In the increasingly organized union movement, at least, First Nations fishers could speak with their own voice and even vote.[37]

The Port Simpson chiefs had already organized a local of the union there before their departure. Machinist Will MacLain, one of the leaders of the BCFU, would soon emerge as the First Nations' main liaison with the union's leadership. The Nelson's Cornet Band was put front and centre in the marches, fundraising tours and rallies to come, when MacLain and the band would combine to draw in the crowds on visits to the coal-mining and fishing towns of the Fraser and south Vancouver Island. MacLain was also one of Vancouver's most prominent socialists.

Soon after their arrival, First Nations fishers from up and down the coast held their first meetings with union leaders, who assured them that a minimum price of twenty-five cents a fish was the non-negotiable demand for the 1900 season. And exclusion of the Nikkei? No doubt many of the union's leaders of all races were firm on that score as well, but first things first: establish a price, win recognition for the union.

The rest would follow. To achieve the price, cooperation with the Nikkei would be a prerequisite.

The chiefs' strategy was fundamentally different from that of the Nikkei. As leaders of the country's First Peoples, the Indigenous leaders were pursuing acknowledgement of their Aboriginal rights and title through direct negotiations with the Crown. As newcomers, the Nikkei were seeking equality in Canadian society. The Indigenous leaders demanded government-to-government acknowledgement of their rights, the Nikkei leaders tried to take their place in the dominant society by winning the right to vote. As a consequence, the Indigenous fishers, particularly the Tsimshian, saw union action as an economic strategy, not as a reflection of their struggle for recognition of rights and title. For the Nikkei, remaining apart from the union was critical. It gave them an organizational basis to defend and expand their place in Canadian society, even if it was at the expense of Indigenous fishers. The unity sought by at least some of the strike's organizations would splinter in the face of this contradiction.

George Kelly, who soon emerged as the voice of the Indigenous fleet, remains an indistinct figure compared to Frank Rogers and Yasushi Yamazaki. Their followers later celebrated their achievements, writing an entire tribute book to Yamazaki and engraving Rogers's fate—"Murdered by a Scab ... Union Organizer and Socialist"—on his tombstone. The silence in the historical record may speak to the weakened state of Aboriginal fishers, to the second-class or racist treatment they experienced in the union, to Kelly's own shortcomings or to all three. Was Kelly white? Was he First Nations? A worker? A chief? In the race-obsessed, class-obsessed province that BC then was, George Kelly's strength may have been that he was all of the above. To white fishermen, he was a voter, more white than Indigenous. To the Tsimshian, he was of noble lineage, but someone who could work in the largely white world with some semblance of equality. To the degree that Kelly combined these contradictory categories, he exemplified what the province was becoming much more than what it had been. He was a charter citizen of the "strange new country" emerging in Steveston.

CHAPTER 3

SOCIALIST VANCOUVER

From the Tsimshian camp on Alexander Street, Kelly's Port Simpson men were only a short walk to any of the spots frequented by the leaders of the newly organized BC Fishermen's Union (formerly the Fraser River Fishermen's Protective and Benevolent Association). The BCFU leaders could have been at the labour council offices at the crest of the hill on Homer Street or at the meeting rooms in a hotel above a bar at 325 Cambie Street, where Vancouver's Socialist Party members held weekly meetings and educationals. They could have been around the corner at the Louvre, 323 Carrall Street, location of "the only circular bar in the province," which advertised prominently in the annual Labour Day program. Boilermaker J.H. Watson, CPR machinist Will MacLain and longshoreman Frank Rogers, all active officers or organizers of the BCFU, were all busy men, deeply involved in the city's frantic labour and political scene. They could be found anywhere at any time.[38]

There was jubilation in the working-class bars of Vancouver's Gastown on the evening of June 9, 1900, when loggers, fishermen, longshoremen and railway workers raised a glass to Will MacLain, first-ever Socialist candidate in a BC provincial election and winner of 4.6 percent of the ballots cast—enough to secure twelfth and last place. MacLain's Socialist platform had won him 648 votes, about one third of the 1,747 received by former premier Joe Martin, the "stormy petrel" of BC politics, who had come second on the "government" slate. Clearly the Socialist vote had been enough to affect the outcome, stripping votes away from candidates who might otherwise have made the cut. Rogers had campaigned tirelessly for MacLain; Watson, a Liberal federally, had supported more mainstream candidates. The top five vote-getters in the city race would go to Victoria, while many of the other candidates would play roles in the events that followed.[39]

No clear provincial victor emerged from the election, but the labour movement had demonstrated new power across the province, electing some veteran union leaders to the legislature and propelling many more centrist candidates across the line. Labour support had obviously been a big factor for two newly minted Vancouver MLAs. They included *News-Advertiser* publisher Francis Carter-Cotton, who held Conservative leanings and ran as a "Provincial Party" candidate—effectively a member of the Opposition—and Liberal pharmacist R.G. Macpherson, who supported "the government." Both were strong advocates of Asiatic exclusion, the key pledge for any candidate seeking labour support and an issue that united left and right.

The election did not end the long political crisis that had paralyzed the legislature during more than three years of corruption allegations, kickback scandals, shifting government majorities and legislative chaos. For the labour movement, it had not been entirely bad news. During the tumultuous proceedings of the previous legislature, union-friendly legislators had been able to trade their votes to implement some important changes, including an eight-hour workday in the mining industry.

But the crisis-ridden government of Charles Semlin had finally collapsed on February 23 due to lack of support. Notable among those not supporting the premier was Joe Martin, his erstwhile attorney general. Lieutenant Governor Thomas McInnes gave Semlin time to find Opposition members who might rally to his side, then suddenly demanded Semlin's resignation on February 27. The legislature condemned his actions by a vote of 22–15. Undeterred, McInnes then called on Martin to form a government. This time, his actions were rejected March 1 by a 28–1 vote of non-confidence in Martin, who had only his own vote on his side. McInnes then prorogued the legislature.

The lieutenant governor's arrival at the legislature triggered a walkout of MLAs led by James Dunsmuir, son of coal baron Robert Dunsmuir. McInnes read his speech to empty benches. Outside, the jeers of the outraged members of the legislature mingled with the cheers and fireworks of citizens celebrating the relief of Ladysmith in South Africa the day before, ending a months-long Boer siege of British forces. Somewhere, on the other side of the world, the DCORs were striking a blow for the Empire, but here at home, no functional government existed.

Joseph Martin was unabashed. The ambitious lawyer felt himself up to the task of premier and did his best to form a new administration, even enlisting non-elected friends and acquaintances to assume cabinet posts. Good friends were hard to find. When Martin called a convention of federal Liberals, hoping to enlist their support, the meeting ended in fisticuffs. His hard work and ingenuity were not enough; by the end of April 1900, Martin was forced to go to the polls. Despite a compelling campaign, the voters returned only twelve members to support Martin's leadership. (It was later revealed that much of Martin's campaign had been underwritten by a railway company seeking major land concessions.)

McInnes had to find yet another premier, turning this time to James Dunsmuir. The new government leader needed weeks to pull together a majority. The confirmation of Dunsmuir as premier did little, however, to create new stability. As one historian concluded, "throughout the province, respect for all constituted authority had suffered a sad eclipse."[40]

In Vancouver, it was widely accepted that "the CPR's the government here." The completion of the railroad had triggered an explosion of investment, particularly in the transportation infrastructure needed to move the province's apparently inexhaustible resources to market. Railway promotions could be launched for next to nothing but were invariably accompanied by lavish land allocations from Victoria. Lumber concessions were available for pennies an acre, mineral rights for royalties that amounted to a minor inconvenience, and salmon were available for the taking. Despite the province's abundant natural wealth, provincial tax revenues were so meagre that provincial debt doubled and tripled during the 1890s. Even the new legislature buildings were debt financed.[41]

Vancouver in 1900 was a wide-open town in a frontier province. Visitors looking out from the top floor of the Hotel Vancouver could still see old-growth timber in any direction.

Squamish First Nation villages were visible on the north shore of Burrard Inlet, the village of Snauq stood at the south entrance of False Creek within sight of the city centre, and the Musqueam had two communities on the Fraser's North Arm, as they had for thousands of years. The city was centred on the CPR railhead on Burrard Inlet, where the transcontinental trains could be unloaded directly across the docks to passenger steamers and freighters headed to every port in the Pacific.

New civic attractions, like the hotel and an opera house, were located here, on the CPR's original land grant, not in the previous town centre around the courthouse on the site of what is now Victory Square. Resource extraction was the province's core business: mining, logging and canning salmon. Railroads and steamship lines linked these resources to market. These were the CPR's domain, but the mines, sawmills and canneries were owned by others. Altogether, only a few score men effectively controlled the provincial economy. The legislature was at best a facilitator, at worst a nuisance, to these investors. In an economic system like BC's, socialist thinking seemed like a statement of the obvious.

Since it was razed by fire in 1886, Vancouver had become both the province's financial centre and its machine shop, generating hundreds of jobs in construction, transportation and manufacturing. It was experiencing exponential growth. The oldest buildings in the bustling downtown core were under twenty years old and the entire city—the rail yards, the retail districts, the industrial areas, city hall, the courts, the hospital and most homes, of both rich and poor—fit comfortably in a fraction of the Burrard Peninsula, bound on both north and south by the CPR rail yards. One freight line cut through the heart of the downtown core.

The hotels of Gastown, built around the original city square next to the port, were home to the loggers, long-shoremen and immigrants passing through the city, including the gold seekers still heading for the Klondike and many more disappointed prospectors returning. Kelly could walk from the Tsimshian camp near the docks, smokestacks and green chains of Hastings Mill, across the Powell Street Grounds where a small Nikkei community was putting down roots, through Chinatown, past the courthouse and then up to the comfortable homes of the West End, where CPR managers enjoyed ocean views from their mansions, in under an hour.

Vancouver's population had doubled between 1891 and 1901 to twenty-seven thousand. Transportation and manufacturing accounted for nearly one-third of all jobs, construction for another 20 percent.[42] Workers with a skilled trade, particularly in key industries like the railway, shipbuilding or other construction had a strong bargaining position and made the most of it. The result was an explosion of union organization that reflected similar changes across the continent.

Vancouver was a hotbed of labour political activity. The more moderate ideology of British union veterans and of American socialist and railway union organizer Eugene Debs was leavened with the more revolutionary perspectives evolving in the industrial cities of the United States. The Vancouver Island coal belt had been a centre of the labour movement for decades, but the boom in hard-rock mining in the Kootenays during the 1890s brought in a new current of militancy as the Western Federation of Miners moved north from Idaho and Montana. In Vancouver, most occupations had a union, from cigar makers and firefighters to barbers and foundry workers, some more radical than others. The labour aristocracy—the skilled trades, like carpenters and machinists—were highly organized. The seasonal, more physical jobs, like longshoring, fishing and many aspects of mining, were much harder to unionize. In many industries, especially mining and fishing, the use of Chinese, Nikkei and Indigenous workers for much of the menial work created a two-tier workforce, one able to bargain and the other virtually powerless.

Watson and MacLain were both railway men, but from opposite ends of the labour spectrum. J.H. Watson, English-born and a dedicated trade unionist, had become a delegate to the labour council as a representative of Debs's American Railway Union in 1895, but went on to help found Vancouver's local of the International Boilermakers and Shipbuilders in 1898. A committed Liberal, Watson believed in moderate trade unionism and deplored the growing American influence on Canada's unions, despite his own union's affiliation to the American Federation of Labour. MacLain was the clear leader of labour's socialist faction. His speaking style, in contrast to his friend Frank Rogers, was more "shout and storm." A veteran of the British labour movement, MacLain had spent many years in the US Navy and either jumped ship or was discharged in Seattle. In Vancouver, he had found work as a machinist in the CPR shops.[43]

MacLain's political ally Rogers may have arrived in Vancouver in 1898 during the gold rush. He described himself as a seaman and lived in a boat on the waterfront, where he worked as a longshoreman, but his early life is a complete mystery. He may be the same twenty-year-old Frank Rogers who immigrated to Canada from Liverpool on the *Circassian* in 1888 with his young bride, Mary. If so, any details of the intervening years are unknown. His death certificate put his year of birth as 1878, although the coroner who performed Rogers's autopsy in 1903 thought him in his thirties. Whatever his background, he quickly impressed his peers. Watson, then president of the labour council, hired him in 1899 to organize the BCFU. By the next spring, Rogers was chairing the city's first May Day meeting and helping to found a new socialist party that won hundreds of votes in that spring's provincial election. MacLain, the raging orator, was the mobilizer and advocate of the two. Rogers was the strategist, the organizer, the thinker.

No pictures of Rogers have survived, although a witness at his 1903 trial described him as slim, mustachioed and of slender build. Since Rogers was sitting in front of this witness, a Nikkei fisherman fingering him for the crime of kidnapping, these scant details are probably reliable. The only other description, offered decades later by fisherman Mike Vidulich, who heard Rogers speak during the 1900 strike, recalled him as "stocky" and "quite short, but broad in the shoulders with a strong, open face and dark hair beginning to grey at the sides." Given the contrast with the courtroom description, perhaps Vidulich was recalling MacLain—no photograph of him has survived either.

Cemetery records say Rogers was American; other accounts guess he was of Scots extraction. A newspaper report claimed after his death that he had a wife and children, but there is no mention of them attending his funeral or on any other occasion. (MacLain's wife was so well known to fishermen that she received a personal vote of thanks at the conclusion of the 1900 negotiations.)[44] Yet Rogers emerged from nowhere to join the front ranks of the city's labour movement. He chaired MacLain's campaign meetings and worked to get out the vote in union households. At some point he had received a broad education that he harnessed to considerable personal talent. He proved adept at letters to the editor, telegrams to politicians and powerful speeches that could change the course of a meeting. Although he had never fished, he quickly won the respect and support of fishermen. He, more than any other, sought to build unity across race lines in the struggle to come.

For Rogers and MacLain, politics and union organizing were a single project, two aspects of the same battle to achieve fundamental social change. In less than six months, they helped launch the fishermen's union, split with the existing socialist political party to launch a new organization, and fought an election campaign. Their biggest project was still to come.[45]

Their first battle was with Arthur Spencer, a Socialist Labour Party (SLP) organizer from Hamilton, Ontario, who had travelled to BC in 1899 to expand the organization. Spencer was working fertile ground. A party convention held in 1900 at a hall on Westminster Avenue (now Main Street) with a red flag flying proudly overhead drew delegates from Nanaimo, New Westminster, Revelstoke, Nelson, Rossland, Delta and Vancouver. They endorsed a program for universal adult suffrage, a two-dollars-a-day minimum wage, a forty-four-hour work week, full medical care and free education to age fourteen. But Spencer's brand of socialism, although strictly non-violent, was built on a rock-hard rejection of reformism—"no compromise, no political trading"—that might soften the misery of workers, render them complacent and thus delay the revolution. From Spencer's perspective, middle-of-the-road trade unionists like Watson were "upholding a platform that is a compromise with cockroach business interests." This was not a message Rogers or MacLain could support and still work in the broader labour movement.[46]

As a result, they broke away from the SLP in November 1899 to form the Vancouver Socialist Club. Spencer and other SLP purists denounced MacLain and Rogers as "kangaroos," ready to jump away from the socialist path to pursue the mirage of reform politics. (The SLP later denied Rogers had ever been a member, making it hard for him to hop away.) By April, MacLain, Rogers and others had launched the United Socialist Labour Party, with its goal of "the emancipation of the working class from landlordism and capitalism."[47] The kangaroos had completed their jump. By the first May Day celebration in Vancouver history, chaired by Rogers, membership had risen to 145. By election day, just five weeks later, MacLain claimed their new party had 250 members and momentum was so strong the USLP had its own hall on Westminster Street. The SLP was effectively finished as a force in BC politics. The USLP, soon renamed the Socialist Party of BC, put down deep roots.[48]

Organizing a socialist party was relatively straightforward compared to organizing the fishing industry. MacLain and Rogers spent weeks during that spring visiting potential members, crossing the Strait of Georgia on occasion to organize fishermen on the east coast of Vancouver Island. It is likely at least some of these trips were to Aboriginal communities like those of the Snuneymuxw, Nanoose or Qualicum First Nations—all were planning to fish the Fraser runs. Until the run was imminent, however, fishermen would remain scattered over dozens of communities on hundreds of kilometres of the coast.

For those without a skill or steady work—the kind of regular hours enjoyed by people like street railway men or postal workers—the salmon industry offered twelve weeks of potentially lucrative employment with payment in cash. Since the early 1890s, when fishermen were paid a flat daily wage rate, the canners had moved to pay piece rates for everything, paying fishermen by the fish and shoreworkers by the case. Those prices could shift by the day or even by the hour, depending on the run of fish. In a glut the prices tumbled, and when packing capacity was overwhelmed, fishermen would be put on limits to cap the number of fish the cannery would take. Fishermen of all races had learned the futility of spontaneous action after a price drop. Only concerted bargaining before the season began stood a chance of establishing a minimum price that reduced the risk of cuts. Once the fish were running, discipline collapsed and the waste of fish stunned even hardened observers. In a heavy run, up to one-third of the fish delivered to the dock was thrown away during processing, equivalent to 10 percent of the catch in 1889.

Salmon gillnetting was dangerous, back-breaking work. The first salmon gillnet fishermen cast their nets, usually fabricated from flax twine by First Nations women, from canoes. By the 1880s, the industry was relying on larger, more stable flat-bottomed skiffs built on the cheap at riverside shipyards. By 1900, the Fraser River fleet had transitioned to much larger round-bottomed, nine-metre boats based on a Columbia River design capable of packing more than two tonnes of salmon. The gillnet skiffs were equipped with a single sail, either sprit- or gaff-rigged, on a stout mast in the boat's bow, but most manoeuvring had to be accomplished by long oars, an almost impossible task against any current or tide. Once towed to the grounds by a cannery tug, the fishermen were on their own for at least twelve hours, casting their four-hundred-metre-long nets over the stern and pulling them back by hand as the boat puller used the long oars to row stern-first along the net. Their only shelter was a partial tent cover over the bow, where the fishermen kept their food and a tin-can stove to boil tea or coffee.

The waters of the Fraser estuary were among the most dangerous on the British Columbia coast. A constantly shifting system of channels, sandbars and tidal flats could quickly be whipped to a chop by winds from any direction. It was a long trip back upstream to the canneries lined along the Fraser's north bank, especially for a laden gillnetter. Many undoubtedly came to grief on dark, windy nights as they blew out of the main channel to the mudflats of the estuary, or worse, the open waters of the Strait of Georgia. No one who became aware of the working conditions confronted by fishermen thought they were overpaid.[49]

In a province where other major resource industries were scattered over thousands of kilometres of rugged wilderness, the salmon industry was unique. Although canneries had spread the length of the coast, the largest share of the catch was canned in the twenty canneries concentrated in the short stretch of the Fraser between Steveston and New Westminster. The Fraser was the largest salmon river in the world, supporting a succession of runs of five species of salmon that began returning to the river in the spring and continued until the early winter. Most abundant of all were the sockeye, prized for their beautiful oily orange flesh, whose runs returned to the great stream-fed lakes in BC's Interior. These runs, beginning in mid-July and peaking in early to mid-August, flooded the canneries.

The time from when a canner organized financing to the ultimate delivery of canned salmon to the retail market in the United Kingdom could take up to two years, a period the canners experienced as fraught with risk and opportunities for disaster. A sudden glut of salmon from Alaska or the Columbia River could drive down export prices long after it was too late for BC canners to make adjustments. As a result, the Fraser canners did everything possible to reduce this risk or transfer it to others. They were the first in the province to adopt assembly-line production techniques, ruthlessly eliminating labour for machinery whenever possible.

Entire sections of the workforce—Indigenous women in the cannery, Chinese workers on the butchering line, Nikkei gillnetters—were put on piece-rate contracts to avoid the liability of paying wages when fish were not running. When the fish were running, however, the balance of power swung back toward the fishers and shoreworkers. There was no profit in a fish that was not caught; it was gone for good. Coal remained to be mined after a strike and trees were still there to be felled, but once the salmon runs had passed, it was too late for the canners.

Vancouver was home to the largest fleet of white seasonal fishermen, who joined the industry for the sockeye fishery and spent the rest of the year working elsewhere. Also fishing seasonally were hundreds of Aboriginal fishers, many of whom migrated to the Fraser during the sockeye run just as their forebears had travelled to the Fraser Canyon to fish. Although they came to the Fraser for commercial gillnetting, most of them undoubtedly fished their home waters for food fish both before and after their weeks on the Fraser. Often fishing alongside them were newly arrived Nikkei fishermen who worked primarily on the sockeye run but had little or no access to other income before or after the sockeye season.

The fourth group of fishermen, scattered in communities along the Fraser from New Westminster to Fort Langley, were the more serious gillnetters. They might farm or log, but fished nearly year-round, from the beginning of the spring salmon runs in late winter to the chum salmon returns in late fall. These fishermen, more powerful politically because of their ability to elect or defeat a member of Parliament in several ridings, were "free fishermen" who were not tied to any particular cannery. They led the battle against the "conservation" schemes hatched by the canners that would tie licences to cannery ownership and limit their numbers.

The result was a mix of open entry, with licences freely available to local white residents, and cannery licences, originally allocated to First Nations fishers but now offered increasingly to Nikkei. The numbers of both types of licence grew steadily during the 1890s, further undermining fishermen's bargaining strength. As if those problems weren't enough, the industry was dominated by the most effective corporate combine in the province.[50]

By 1893, Henry Bell-Irving had tapped his family network in the United Kingdom to raise the funds necessary to complete the merger of many of the province's canneries into the Anglo-British Columbia Packing Co. Bell-Irving became the effective leader of the canners and an expert at exploiting the divisions among the fishermen, ensuring that their halting attempts at organization never resulted in an enduring fishermen's organization. The canners further consolidated their position by investing in salmon traps, most on the American side of the boundary, which produced enormous catches without any fishermen whatsoever.

Although these runs were available to Canadian canners once they arrived in Canadian waters, Canadian fishermen were prohibited from delivering south of the boundary. This had the effect of eliminating competition from American buyers, who had access to ample supplies of trap-caught fish in any case. American canneries on Puget Sound, some with ties to Canadian canners, began processing a larger and larger share of the Fraser catch, probably eliminating smaller early- and late-season sockeye runs altogether. It was clear to some fishermen, Rogers among them, that the traps represented a greater threat to BC salmon and the runs themselves than the Nikkei fleet. The American traps not only helped to depress prices, but also posed a deadly threat to conservation of the runs, despite their weekly closures.

Throughout 1899, the fishing industry had been rife with rumours about a renewed canners' combine to hold down the price of sockeye. Support for the union movement was at an all-time high; Debs himself had visited Vancouver to inaugurate the new labour temple on Hornby Street. As news of the canners' efforts was confirmed, fishermen responded in Vancouver and New Westminster by reorganizing the union locals that had fallen into inactivity after the defeats of the previous seven years. But the fishermen were well aware that a new strategy was required if they were to overcome the canners' new unity. It would not be enough for each section of the fleet—white, Indigenous, Nikkei—to issue appeals to each other and hope for the best.

By the spring of 1900, BC fishermen knew they desperately needed a new strategy to protect their incomes. As a larger and larger share of the Fraser runs were taken by American traps, continued expansion of the BC fleet was cutting into incomes on the Canadian side of the line. If the Canadian fishermen continued splintering along race lines, their fate was certain. Sometime in that hectic spring of 1900, fishermen took a dramatic step to avert that possibility.

In March, Watson helped the new BC Fishermen's Union secure a charter from the American Federation of Labor. On March 2, with reports of the terrible Battle of Paardeberg in South Africa still coming in and Vancouver's attention fixed on the desperate siege of Ladysmith, where British forces had just achieved victory, the Vancouver fishermen formally launched their new union with a historic decision: to enroll all fishermen regardless of race, welcoming Aboriginal and Nikkei fishermen into membership on an equal basis with whites.

Despite overwhelming support for Asiatic exclusion among working people, some union organizers, especially socialists, had been advocating for organizing on the basis of full racial equality for years. There were a few short-lived experiments with the strategy, particularly in the mining belt. Time and again, however, economic pressure from employers broke the tenuous solidarity of white and Chinese workers.

The divisions among workers in the fishing industry were significant. Both First Nations and Nikkei fishermen were engaged through a contract labour system that made them dependent on a single boss for pre-season advances as well as access to gear and living quarters during the fishery. They were not free to make alternate arrangements. There were major language barriers and all canneries maintained segregated housing for whites, First Nations, Chinese and Nikkei.

Yet strikes had occurred on many occasions in every section of the industry. Chinese salmon butchers had often shut down production to resolve an immediate grievance, as had Chinese underground workers in the coal mines. First Nations workers not only struck on many occasions but even packed up and went home when conditions on seasonal jobs proved unsatisfactory. The Bows and Arrows, a Vancouver longshore gang made up of Squamish First Nation dock workers, were strong supporters of waterfront union organizers. Nikkei fishermen, although a factor in BC's industry only during the past ten years, had struck for better prices on several occasions. No doubt many of them had seen or participated in union organizing in their home country, where industrialization was proceeding at breakneck speed.

The inaugural issue of *The Independent*, a new labour paper launched in Vancouver on March 31, 1900, showed how far outside the labour mainstream the BCFU was heading. An "Analysis of Mongol Statistics" was a lead feature, a lengthy treatise that concluded 25 percent of the working men in the province were Chinese or Nikkei. "The total exclusion of Oriental cheap labour is the solution to the vexed question," the unnamed author concluded. A possible clue to his identity lay in the list of labour council executive members, including "statistician" Will MacLain.

Despite the fact that support for Asiatic exclusion was the overwhelming view of organized labour, the BCFU proposed a contrary course for price bargaining. The decision to organize fishers of all races in the BC Fishermen's Union was fundamentally a pragmatic one. Throughout the crisis to come, white and First Nations leaders continued to clamour for expulsion of the Nikkei. But as Rogers said later, the fishermen couldn't win without the support of the Nikkei. The price increase was the priority; exclusion would come later, through political action. But if the union achieved recognition from the canners in the form of a negotiated price agreement, how could it then demand expulsion of a large share of its members?

The First Nations fishers, reduced to a minority interest in the industry in just ten years by the steady inclusion of more Nikkei, had a different perspective. A decent price was an important, immediate objective, but an even more critical goal was their survival as participants in the commercial sockeye fishery. The fundamental difference between white fishermen and others was obvious: only white fishermen had the vote. Racism undermined the union's unity even as the organizers—some of them, at least—seemed determined to overcome it. The white fishermen, all voters, could exert political leverage and even launch their own political parties. The Indigenous and Nikkei fishers could neither vote nor gain access to the sockeye fishery without the help of third parties.

For the white fishermen, a decent price was enough; for that, they needed unity. The Nikkei fishermen could not afford to lose. Their challenge was to achieve the best price possible without jeopardizing their long-term future in the industry. Ultimately, they would need to win the vote and they knew it. Indigenous fishers also needed a better price, but protection of their place in the industry was critical. For this they relied on an alliance with the white fishermen, focusing on legal appeals to maintain their Aboriginal rights.

Indigenous fishers had been quick to support the BCFU, forming their own local in Port Simpson late in 1899. The presence of strong First Nations locals in other communities—Nanaimo and Cowichan are often mentioned—was another demonstration of First Nations' political power within the union. How First Nations leaders coordinated their efforts is unclear, although chiefs from a number of coastal communities gathered in Chilliwack in the spring of 1901 to prepare for that season. The coast-wide gatherings every autumn in the Fraser Valley's hop fields may have provided another opportunity for coordination.

As a result of the BCFU's inclusion policy, both Nikkei and Indigenous fishers were present at the union's first meeting in Vancouver. By March 24, the fishermen's overall leadership was in place. Captain J.L. Anderson was elected president, Rogers became vice-president and Watson, who now was a customs officer at his day job, was named secretary. The provincial election continued to dominate the city's political life for the next six weeks, but Rogers moved quickly to strengthen the union's organization when he wasn't chairing election meetings for MacLain. On April 21, Rogers was named secretary of a new joint board created to coordinate the Vancouver and New Westminster locals, and a week later he headed to Steveston with an interpreter to meet with the Nikkei fishermen. By June, he had moved to Steveston nearly full-time. If Kelly or anyone else wanted to find him, that was the place to look. One of Rogers's first appointments must have been with the leaders of Dantai, the new Nikkei fishermen's organization.[51]

CHAPTER 4

JAPANESE STEVESTON

The leaders of the Japanese, or Nikkei, fishermen were already well advanced in their preparations for the salmon season by the time the 1900 provincial election was underway. Their goal was much more than a decent salmon price. They were seeking equality and security in their new homeland. After a decade of a few hundred immigrants a year, by the turn of the new century the flow of Nikkei to Canada soared to hundreds arriving each month, some on their way to the United States, others ready to settle in British Columbia. The founders of the Nikkei community saw the chance to put down roots, but they were determined to do so on their own terms. Community pioneers like thirty-five-year-old Tomekichi Homma, who had already lived in the province for seventeen years, realized that the only certain path to equality was the right to vote. Security would come through a stable community, symbolized by the construction of a hospital and a school.

Manzo Nagano, the first Nikkei immigrant to fish the Fraser, had arrived only twenty-three years before, returning to Japan several times before establishing a salt salmon business in New Westminster in 1894. In 1883, he was followed by Homma, then an eighteen-year-old from Ichikawa Prefecture, and five years later by Gihei Kuno from Wakayama, who returned to Japan to recruit scores more. Until Kuno's initiative, there were fewer than one hundred men on the coast working in the fishing and pelagic sealing industries.

By the time Homma arrived, the future site of Steveston was a riverside farm owned by Manoah Steves, who had purchased the land five years earlier. It was a wild and beautiful place. The western edge of Lulu Island, on which Steveston lay, was defined by a ridge crowned with Pacific crab-apples, wild roses, bitter cherry and Indian plum; a wild grass prairie stretched inland until it met a mixed forest of spruce, cedar, alder and yew. The lowlands and estuary flats were alive with birds, especially in spring and fall when clouds of seabirds or migrating geese filled the sky. Garry Point, where the Fraser's main arm spilled onto the estuary, was marked for many years by a single tall spruce tree, an important landmark for mariners navigating the shifting main channel.

At the Sand Heads, where the main arm of the Fraser finally emptied into the Strait of Georgia, the federal authorities had financed the construction of a fifty-foot hexagonal lighthouse perched on iron pilings and topped with a Fresnel lens. It was a hardship posting, even for the hardiest lightkeepers, who watched ice floes and massive trees sweep by during the spring freshet and nearly went mad ringing the bell during long spells of autumn fog.

Many of the original Nikkei fishermen had arrived on pelagic sealing schooners that had worked their way from ports in Japan around the Pacific Rim, harvesting migrating seals at sea and raiding their Aleutian rookeries before bringing the furs to market in Victoria. (The fleet could then continue on its way south and west, ultimately delivering in Canton.) Some of the sealers spent the winters in Steveston, where the Nikkei found winter work building gillnetters. From there it was an easy step to the job of boat puller, rowing the heavy Fraser gillnet skiffs against wind and tide while the fishermen worked the net. But growth in the Nikkei community was slow. In 1891 only fifty-three Nikkei, including two women, were listed in a permanent population of five hundred, of which about half were Caucasians. The rest were Chinese. By 1900, the permanent Nikkei population was four hundred, of which forty-six were women and twenty-three were children.[52]

The salmon industry, however, grew much faster than the village of Steveston. The permanent population in the late 1880s was about 350, but an estimated ten thousand thronged the community in salmon season, jammed in bunkhouses, hotels or even shanties on the beach. There were three churches, but bars, gambling joints and brothels were constructed even more quickly. The only source of drinking water was the river, and the Nikkei fishermen built a clinic, later a hospital, to treat victims of typhus in 1895.[53]

This Nikkei community in Steveston was just the core of a much larger group of men who used Vancouver and Steveston as way stations on their way elsewhere, usually to the United States. Revolutionary economic and political changes in Japan drove a wave of migration across the Pacific. Hundreds found their way into the fishing industry, many of whom had never been close to a net in their lives. This was a dramatic and very visible change in an industry that had been dominated by First Nations fishers and a few whites since its inception. This influx was welcomed by the canners, who could secure a fisherman's services for the season simply by advancing minimal supplies of rice and fishing gear. Every part of the fishing outfit was rented: boat, oars, corks, net, lead line, sails. The entire cost had to be repaid from the catch. Nikkei fishermen started the season with a significant debt to the canner; they had to fish their way to a pay day.[54]

Nikkei fishermen lived in primitive conditions, with thirty to sixty "boys"—many were still in their teens—lodged in the bunkhouse of a "boss" who earned a commission on the catch landed by his charges and nego-tiated on their behalf with the cannery. Drinking untreated river water, eating a meagre rice and fish diet, crowded in smoky bunkhouses with bunks stacked three high, the Nikkei fishermen were vulnerable to disease. Typhus, a fever spread by ticks and lice, took a serious toll, as did beriberi, a wasting disease caused by thiamine deficiency, often related to a diet of polished or husked rice. The prev-alence of these diseases drove community leaders to build the small hospital.

The Nikkei fishermen were subject to a form of inden-tured labour, working at odd jobs as shingle or net makers in the off-season, drinking and gambling with their fellow workers to while away the time. "None of the men had wives then," one house boss recalled. "And as there were no women, they'd get wild. Just a few drinks and they'd start a fight ... some men killed each other, some were put in jail." Sanitation was primitive, despite the deep wooden bathtubs outside the uninsulated bunkhouses, heated with Fraser driftwood.[55]

The surge in immigration was driven in part by a plague outbreak in Hawaii, where many migrants had hoped to settle or transship to California. With the Hawaiian Islands closed by quarantine, the cheapest alternative was

Vancouver, a convenient waypoint to the United States. In Japan, the authorities issued passports freely to anyone who applied. In one notorious fraud, several thousand stolen passports, complete with false official stamps, were sold all over Japan. Immigration agents often arranged the trips, charging an upfront commission fee and washing their hands of their customers the moment they left Japanese waters. The newcomers were often penniless on arrival in Vancouver, lacking even the seventy-five cents necessary to travel on to Seattle. "These poor people were flowing into Steveston like schools of salmon in the Fraser River," recalled one veteran. "The small village of Steveston saw its ranks swell suddenly to four thousand Japanese versus the existing community of four thousand whites. This sudden influx naturally created racial tension." In contrast, the resident white community numbered only a few hundred.

By 1897, Nikkei fishermen had concluded they needed an organization, not only to represent them in bargaining but also to create the basis for a true Nikkei community in Steveston. Dantai, later called the Japanese Fishermen's Benevolent Association, was the result. Among the founders of the new organization were Homma and Kamekichi Ohki.[56]

The increase in Nikkei immigrants proved a huge challenge for the "old-time Japanese." The newcomers were young and restless, unfamiliar with fishing or Canada. By 1899, new arrivals to the province totalled nearly nine thousand men. From a few hundred fishermen four years earlier, the Nikkei fleet had grown to nearly two thousand in 1900. The original health-care centre created in 1896 by Methodist missionaries to treat victims of typhus would need a significant expansion. The Dantai executive allocated $1,800 for the task, a very large sum for their poverty-stricken community. Care was available to all, without discrimination.[57]

In 1899, Nikkei community leaders decided to reorganize Dantai to reflect their broader goals. The purposes of the new Japanese Fishermen's Benevolent Association, finally incorporated in June 1900, were threefold: to promote the interests of Nikkei engaged in the fisheries; to build, equip and maintain both a hospital and then a school; and "to maintain and foster good understanding between the Japanese and Cannerymen."[58] Given the presence of Nikkei bosses in the leadership—Ohki seems to have been particularly influential—the goal of good relations with the canners was revealing. In part, it was a practical statement of the reality that without good relations, the existence of the Nikkei community would be at risk. On the other hand, the canners and the Nikkei did not have the same interests. Nikkei fishermen needed higher prices as badly as the white fishermen did, a direct conflict with the objectives of the canners and their agents, the Nikkei house bosses. The reorganization of Dantai had both practical and political goals. Negotiating a better share of the salmon industry's profits was one.

Homma, now a naturalized British subject, had an even longer-term strategy to empower the Nikkei—a legal challenge to force authorities to grant the Nikkei the vote. But executing this complex legal strategy would make it impossible for him to remain at the helm of Dantai. The organization needed new leadership in what was expected to be a tumultuous salmon season. Homma wanted to step back from the leadership to pursue his quest to achieve the franchise for Nikkei immigrants. Full citizenship, including the right to vote, was the key to success in Canadian society and the only way the Nikkei could hope to offset the political clout of those, including white fishermen, who wished to marginalize or expel them.

The other likely candidate, although a capable accountant, was too quiet for the confrontations the Dantai leadership expected. Although 98 percent of the new arrivals were literate, most were still in their teens or early twenties and knew nothing of fishing or of British Columbia. They needed someone more forceful than an accountant to lead them, ideally a "brawler and a drinker." The call went out to Yasushi Yamazaki; he would be perfect.[59]

Yamazaki, then only thirty years old, had several careers already behind him that uniquely qualified him for the drama to come. Born in Toyama in May 1870, he was the third son of a samurai family. Toyama was isolated and impoverished. Its small fishing communities faced west to the Sea of Japan, with steep, forest-covered mountains at their backs. The mountains, the trees and the rushing rivers all had their parallels in British Columbia, where Yamazaki would spend much of his life.

As a child, Yamazaki learned to read Chinese and calligraphy at an old-fashioned Buddhist school. In 1884, at the age of fourteen, he decided to leave home, although why is unclear. The decision was fateful. He walked the four hundred kilometres from Toyama to Tokyo, travelling for at least nine days. His goal was to live in the home of his teacher's second son. With no money for tuition, Yamazaki was forced to study on his own. One of his mentors found him a job as a night watchman at a Tokyo newspaper, where he spent many hours reading the books that had been sent in to the newspaper for reviews.[60]

In 1888, then only eighteen, he sailed for San Francisco. Soon after his arrival, he enrolled in English studies with an instructor who had graduated from Keio University, then signed on for a three-year stint as a seaman in the US Navy aboard the fifteen-hundred-ton *Mohican*, a square-rigger equipped with auxiliary steam engines. The pay of sixteen dollars a month was attractive enough, but Yamazaki also took advantage of two hours of daily English instruction offered on board by the chaplain.

Soon after Yamazaki enlisted, probably in late 1889 or early 1890, the *Mohican* began a tour of the Pacific and in 1893 returned to Honolulu to support American interests seeking to depose Queen Lili'uokalani, the Islands' monarch. Yamazaki was a witness to the overthrow of Queen Lili'uokalani and the ultimate annexation of Hawaii to the United States.

Although his three-year service contract must have been nearly at an end, Yamazaki later told astonishing tales of his efforts to be discharged, dishonourably if nothing else worked. Bad behaviour led to repeated trips to the brig, where he claimed a Chinese steward smuggled alcohol to him through a hose. Despite his work skills, which he believed engendered special tolerance from his officers, he finally secured dismissal. "As a last resort, I beat up the officer who favoured me most with an iron bar," he said later, "then, finally, they dropped me off at Honolulu. On the discharge papers, it said that I was very healthy but my behaviour was very bad. It was a reasonable statement but I ripped it up as I walked down the steps from the boat." When work proved unavailable in Honolulu, he returned to San Francisco. Whatever happened to simple desertion? Combative, stubborn and always ready for violence: those were qualities that defined Yamazaki, an individualist who saw himself as someone special, a leader of men, perhaps a samurai.[61]

On his return to San Francisco, Yamazaki opened an inn on Brannan Street catering to Nikkei sailors. Innkeeping was only one of his occupations. He also worked as an apprentice engineer at the Union Iron Factory and continued his education at night school. The owner of Union Iron, impressed by Yamazaki, helped him find work as an engineer aboard the steamer *Grand Holmes*, which was shipping canned salmon to Scotland from British Columbia. But Yamazaki's penchant for conflict again became evident. After a fight with his ship's officer, he quit the *Grand Holmes* in Nanaimo where it had stopped for coal. It proved a lucky decision: the *Grand Holmes* was soon shipwrecked in Patagonia and the surviving crew members were massacred by the locals.

Yamazaki made his way to Victoria, where he found work as a cook aboard the forty-five-ton sealing schooner *Cedar Table*. There were about two hundred Nikkei sailors and hunters in the city, including the famous seal shooter Shotaro Shimizu. In the twenty years before and after the turn of the century, sealers from the United States, Canada and Japan pursued the migrating seal herds to the Bering Sea. Canadian vessels travelled from east to west, but Nikkei vessels worked the coast in the opposite direction, or picked up the herds on the high seas and made a stop in Victoria. These Nikkei sealers, comfortable in the small rowing skiffs that were dropped from the schooner in pursuit of the seals, were to form the nucleus of BC's Nikkei salmon fishing fleet by the late 1880s. Their numbers were bolstered by immigrants from Wakayama, where poverty and declining fish stocks were driving out members of that region's ancient fishing communities.[62]

In December 1893, the *Cedar Table* set out for Japan, harrying the seals as they migrated north to the Aleutians. Jack London's *Sea Wolf*, the fictional tale of a similar schooner's cruise published in 1904, graphically describes the hardships of the sealing fleet based on London's own cruise a few years before. After hours and days in a small skiff on the open ocean, often miles from the mother ship, the hunters would shoot and land their prey before awaiting recovery by the schooner. Then came more days of butchering the seals, knee-deep in blood and gore on the pitching schooner deck, before salting the hides for storage.

The crew of the *Cedar Table* crossed the Pacific and returned to Victoria in just ten months, taking Yamazaki back to the port of Yokohama from which he had sailed six years earlier. If *Cedar Table*'s crew was like the majority based in Victoria, Yamazaki's shipmates were Nuu-chah-nulth hunters picked up from their Ahousaht and Clayoquot homes as the schooner headed west. Chinook, the fur traders' language that was the lingua franca of the BC coast, was undoubtedly the main language spoken on board. The young Yamazaki, familiar with Chinese and fluent in Japanese and English, could also communicate easily with members of BC's First Nations.[63]

After this epic cruise, Yamazaki travelled to Port Essington, working as a fisherman, logger and construction labourer. His engineering experience proved useful to Nikkei carpenter Zentaro Fujuwara, who was undertaking winter refits on the Hudson's Bay Company's riverboats *Hazelton* and *Mount Royal* in Port Simpson. It is possible Yamazaki crossed George Kelly's path during these years.

Yamazaki later recalled his Skeena days with affection:

> Sometimes we did reckless things. We tried to raise the price of sockeye to eight cents from six cents per fish. We Nikkei fishermen were leading the strike but white and native fishermen seemed to be breaking the strike and going fishing. So, we decided to beat them up. We waited for them at a scow camp near the Skeena River, ready to fight. Seven or eight fishing

boats came along with white fishermen at the helm. We beat them up, ripped their nets, and damaged their cannery boats.

Yamazaki and eleven others were quickly arrested and held in the tiny Port Essington lockup, where they awaited trial by local cannery managers who acted as justices of the peace. Ringleader Mankichi Sakai was sentenced to six months in jail, the others fined twenty-five dollars. Yamazaki, however, travelled to Victoria with Sakai and succeeded in overturning the conviction on appeal, arguing that the Port Essington cannery bosses had no legal authority. The judge agreed, noting that the "municipality" of Port Essington did not exist. Yamazaki would soon put these experiences to good use.

By 1898, Yamazaki was ready to follow the gold rush to the Klondike. He spent time in Skagway, acting as an armed guard in a gambling den, then moved even farther north to an isolated gold-mining town called Sunrise on Cook Inlet. After a winter of extreme hardship, he walked seventy miles to the cannery at the inlet's mouth to catch a ship leaving for San Francisco, which dropped him at Seattle. It was 1899. It was there the Steveston fishermen caught up to him. They needed help: a brawler, someone who could speak English and Chinook, familiar with salmon fishing, unafraid to stand up to vested interests of any sort. Would he help? Yes, he would. In Dantai's new corporate documents, Iwakichi Kimamura was president, Ohki remained as vice-president and Yamazaki became secretary.

CHAPTER 5

THE 1900 STRIKE

On April 28, 1900, Frank Rogers hired a Nikkei interpreter and took the stagecoach to Steveston. He was constantly on the move during the following weeks, often joined by a changing committee of rank-and-file fishermen who undertook negotiations with the Nikkei and the canners. Rogers met with anyone he could, including canner C.S. Windsor, who walked the longshoreman through his books. Whatever his background, the thirty-year-old Rogers clearly had outstanding leadership abilities: campaign manager, organizer, negotiator, propagandist and strategist. By the spring of 1900 he had risen to vice-president of the BCFU.

By May 12, Rogers was able to meet with the Nikkei bosses, men at least as influential as the Dantai leaders in directing the Nikkei fleet. (Many were also Dantai activists.) Among the Nikkei fishermen were industry veterans who had a history in the fishery and understood its workings. Rogers and the other BCFU leaders regarded these "old-time Japs" as key to an alliance with the Nikkei fleet and therefore crucial to the success of bargaining. The Nikkei held about half the licences and had sufficient capacity to keep the canneries working in the event of a strike.

The BCFU proposed a single organization of all fishermen, but if that wasn't possible, they would consider alternative ways to pressure the canners. Initial responses seemed encouraging. Nikkei leaders wanted a fixed price for salmon and were prepared to cooperate. They refused to join the BCFU, but kept the door open for joint negotiations. In the meantime, however, they began their own discussions with the Bell-Irvings' Fraser River Canners' Association. By late June, with the provincial election finally over, there were reports that the Nikkei had rejected an offer of fifteen cents a fish. It seemed the Nikkei leadership was prepared to insist on twenty-five cents a fish assuming moderate runs and a catch of about one thousand fish per boat for the season. Despite these developments, the BCFU leaders continued to hold out hope for a single fishermen's bargaining association, across racial lines, that would be recognized by the canners.

The Nikkei leadership pursued their strategy with impressive energy and discipline, particularly after Yasushi Yamazaki accepted his assignment. Throughout the spring, they worked feverishly to rewrite the constitution and bylaws of the Japanese Fishermen's Benevolent Association to reflect their broader community goals, not just their objectives in the salmon fishery. Under the circumstances, it should have come as no surprise to the BCFU fishermen that their proposal for a single organization could be dead on arrival. Their hopes may have been sustained by the fact that prominent members of the Nikkei fleet were vocally supporting a single organization—presumably the BCFU—fearing that rejection would prove fatal to the community's aspirations.

Writing a generation later, strike veteran Takejiro Ooide, a strong supporter of Yamazaki, described the tensions:

> ... the establishment of the Japanese Fishermen's Association was a clear act of hostility towards white fishermen, under the circumstances. Therefore, some people, such as Captain Hayashi and Sino-Japanese war heroes Sergeant Fukushima and Corporal Nimune strongly objected to it. If Japanese fishermen were defeated by white fishermen and had to leave the fishing grounds, many Japanese wouldn't be able to make a living and might simply starve. The hard-liners insisted that this was a matter of survival and we had to fight against racist expulsion by any means. This point of view won majority support, fortunately.[64]

The dissenters who had objected to the reorganization of Dantai were met with iron discipline. Yamazaki "set up a private court to judge people who disrupted the common front. Some people were fined and some were expelled. This could not have been done if not for Yamazaki."[65] Yamazaki's big stick was accompanied by a carrot calculated to win the support of the restless, hungry and ambitious young men who made up the bulk of the membership. As a veteran of the seal fishery and the Skeena salmon fishery, he knew how to curry favour with the rank and file, "rough people who not only loved to drink, gamble and buy sex, but also loved to fight. Yamazaki could fight and drink with them, but he did not gamble or buy sex. Still, he found it necessary to create a gambling house to accommodate those people.

Subsequently, he sat with a gun on the desk of the Japanese Fishermen's Association, ready to talk about their mission with anyone." Men who didn't support Dantai were welcome to carouse elsewhere—and may have been forced to do so at gunpoint.[66]

Although they could not know it at the time, the Dantai majority's victory would not endure. This "act of hostility," combined with Dantai's subsequent strategy, may not have doomed the Nikkei community to expulsion in 1942, but it undermined those, both in the Nikkei fleet and the white union leadership, who were seeking a different direction. The Dantai leadership's decision was pragmatic and needed to be ruthlessly enforced, given the rising campaign for Asiatic exclusion. They were ready to collaborate with the union, but not to disappear into its ranks.

Two key groups heading into salmon bargaining—the Nikkei and the First Nations fleets—were seeking to consolidate their place in the industry. In effect, they were seeking to do so at each other's expense, although there is nothing on record to suggest the Nikkei sought the expulsion of First Nations. For the white fishermen, many of whom were using the salmon fishery as a source of supplemental or seasonal income, the issue was strictly economic. Their place in the industry was secure.[67]

Yamazaki worked at a frantic pace. Soon after his arrival in Steveston, Dantai had mobilized the fishermen to begin building the new hospital under the supervision of a Yokohama carpenter named Oota. Fishermen agreed to contribute labour. Lumber was secured from a sympathetic lumberyard operator in New Westminster. Because BC law prohibited discrimination by hospital operators, a white doctor and nurses had to be hired. Donations were sought all over the region and ultimately a large loan was required from senior members of the community. The debt incurred was significant, probably more than $1,000, and would play an important role in the negotiations to come. The new hospital quickly took shape, a tangible symbol of the Nikkei community's determination to sink deep roots in Steveston. With that project in hand, Yamazaki began more detailed discussions with the union.[68]

Behind the scenes, Henry Bell-Irving and the canners were still doing their own calculations. On June 23, they agreed among themselves to fix a price, but deferred a decision on the precise amount or the timing. They were unanimous that they would not negotiate with the BCFU. When Rogers asked association secretary W.A. Duncan for a meeting, he was firmly rebuffed, although a delegation of fishermen did get a hearing the next day, apparently on the basis they were not formally representing the union. Three days later, the canners met again, this time secretly fixing the price at twenty cents a fish and agreeing to fund the wages of three special police. Duncan quietly made arrangements for three men, picked by the canners, to be sworn as provincial constables at the canners' expense. The canners now focused their energies on achieving a settlement with the Nikkei. This alone, they believed, would be effective to break any strike, just as it had been in previous years.[69]

The contrast between the meetings of the canners and the fishermen could hardly have been more stark. The canners, all men of substantial means, united by their pursuit of profit, met in panelled downtown offices. Duncan was hired to issue bulletins and brief reporters, to telegraph worried demands to Ottawa and Victoria, and to retain Pinkerton detectives as required. The fishermen, who met both at the Dantai office in Steveston and at the BCFU office on Vancouver's Westminster Avenue, came from every part of the world and were pursuing very different objectives. How they convened their meetings or made decisions is not known, but the negotiations, which probably required translators fluent in Japanese, English and Chinook, quickly increased in frequency and intensity. Gathered around the table were white fishermen, many of British descent, Nikkei fishers and Indigenous leaders. Apart from the Indigenous leaders, few of the fishermen had been more than ten years in the industry, many only three or four. Most were in their twenties and thirties.

Captain J.L. Anderson, Rogers, MacLain and Watson—all skilled workers, three of whom had significant maritime experience—were the main voices for the BCFU, but the two socialists, MacLain and Rogers, would be the most prominent. Although MacLain and Yamazaki came from opposite sides of the globe, they had some things in common. Both had served in the US Navy and both had experience in the metal trades. Although little is known about Anderson's career, he was probably the same J.L. Anderson who later skippered a sealing schooner out of Victoria. In the small world of the pelagic sealing fleet, which numbered under twenty vessels, it is probable he had also crossed paths with Yamazaki.

Was George Kelly present along with other chiefs, like Squamish Chief Joe Capilano? First Nations fishers, after all, had been the original Fraser harvesters, both in the pre-contact era and with the rise of the canning industry. Both Yamazaki and Kelly were familiar with the waters of the Skeena and had spent time in the tiny community of Port Simpson, or Lax Kw'alaams. Did they acknowledge this connection? Kelly is not mentioned in news reports of various fishermen's delegations, although he was a fixture at BCFU rallies and marches, speaking on several occasions. It is hard to imagine that First Nations chiefs would delegate responsibility for bargaining to the white fishermen, given their bitter experiences in other salmon strikes. The Port Simpson men, after all, had organized their own union local.

Then there were the Nikkei, some of whom had been in the industry as long as their white counterparts. Surely, in an industry as concentrated as the salmon fishery, where fishers often set their nets just metres apart from one another in the midst of a fleet numbering hundreds of boats, they had at least some acquaintances among the white gillnetters. Dantai's leaders were not novices at price bargaining. The Nikkei bosses had quick access to the canners and did their best to push for a settlement that would protect their investments and ensure a basic income for their boys.

These men, from such different backgrounds, now found themselves organizing together in this "strange new country." These were the ancestral territories of the First Nations, but transformed by their own experience of contact and colonialism. Many, like the Tsimshian, were far from home as well. The others were true newcomers, from every part of the globe, some free to come and go but others determined, even desperate, to settle. In Steveston, for the duration of the salmon season, they were thrown together without the firm hand of the white power structure to keep them in check. In the political chaos of this moment in British Columbia, they saw an opportunity. They had more in common than they expected.

Yamazaki, with his command of English, Japanese and Chinook, was uniquely situated to influence the course of events; he remained unswervingly committed to his members' mandate. Yamazaki's job was neither easy nor pleasant. Ooide remembered the virulent racism that was a fact of the Nikkei fishermen's lives. "In those days, white labourers looked down on Nikkei labourers like dirt and did not treat them like human beings," he wrote. "Yamazaki went alone to the Labour Hall, the home of the Canadian labour union[s], attended the meetings with dignity and engaged in honourable discussions ... It was heroism of a do-or-die nature." Yamazaki's skill with his fists was not in doubt, but he also demonstrated "skillful diplomacy."[70]

Yamazaki mixed diplomacy with some blunt talk. He was quick to point out that most of the white fishermen were seasonal harvesters, there for the sockeye and gone when it ended. "When Yamazaki negotiated with the white fishermen's union, he often pointed out this issue," Ooide recalled, "and said, 'Most of you are not professional fishermen. Our Japanese fishermen are professionals, who have been fishing for many years in this country and some of us had fishing backgrounds even in Japan. Why don't you let our professionals handle the price negotiation?' He explained, reasonably, how absurd the white fishermen's demands were and refuted their logic. Because their real intentions were nothing to do with the price of fish, they didn't listen to his reasoning."

Given the reality—that most Nikkei fishermen had been in the country less than three years and often relied on dubious immigration documents—this approach was not likely to win friends. The reference to the union's "real intentions" is probably a reflection of the view among some Nikkei bosses that the union was more interested in socialist revolution than price bargaining. It is possible, however, that Yamazaki's exploits on the Skeena, where he was fighting strikebreakers to raise the price, gave him added credibility with the union men.

It fell to Rogers and MacLain, but particularly to Rogers, to bridge the divides. Rogers did the exhausting and tedious work of building relationships wherever and whenever he could: with canners, Nikkei fishermen, First Nations leaders and even, as later events would show, with the police. He knew Yamazaki did not speak for all Nikkei fishermen. Throughout the dispute, Rogers was able to find Nikkei fishers to interpret, assist on picket duty and argue for greater unity between the union and Nikkei fleets.

The discussions between the BCFU and Dantai went back and forth. From the Nikkei perspective, it seemed impossible to find an agreeable price. When the Nikkei suggested a number, the BCFU leadership would propose five cents a fish higher. But Ooide confirms that the Dantai leadership ultimately supported a twenty-five-cent price demand, whatever discussions preceded it. This was the price the strike would be fought on. It made sense for the BCFU to accept that proposal; anything higher would end the strike before it began by wrecking the fragile united front they were seeking to build with the Nikkei. Rogers later told a special committee of the legislature that he had written up an agreement between the BCFU and Dantai recording the agreement on a twenty-five-cent demand: "They said they would stand firm with the union until the canners proved to the whole of us that they could not afford to pay twenty-five cents; and then, probably, we would come to some other agreement." This was careful language. Twenty-five cents would be an opening position, not a final one.[71]

There was no time to lose. Fishing would normally begin in early July—the season formally opened July 1—and build to a climax as the run peaked later that month. But rather than stop the fishery after the run had begun, both the BCFU and Dantai leaders preferred to determine a new price before any nets went in the water. It would be much easier to keep the fleet tied up than to persuade fishermen to pick up their nets once the fish were running.

Late in June, Watson joined Rogers in Steveston for a key meeting with Nikkei leaders at their invitation. The Nikkei introduced the Dantai leadership—Kimamura, Ohki and Yamazaki—as counterparts of Anderson, Watson and Rogers, declaring that Dantai and the BCFU had the same objectives on salmon prices. They suggested a joint strategy to achieve twenty-five cents a fish, although the details of that strategy have not survived. Watson later defined this meeting as the point at which the BCFU leadership finally accepted that the Nikkei and other fishermen would not work in a single organization, despite their shared concern to achieve a better price. Although the BCFU reiterated its call for all fishermen to join under its banner, the largest Nikkei organization in the province, claiming some 1,250 members, refused to do so.

The only account of this pivotal encounter was later provided by Watson in a letter to the *Vancouver Daily World*. Given the people involved, the significance of the meeting must have been clear to all present. Were Kelly or other First Nations leaders in the room? The record is silent. The BCFU leadership was dismayed by the refusal of Dantai to merge its membership with BCFU. "It is not for want of trying the Japs are not members of the BC Fishermen's Union," Watson said later. "The Japs were the first to ask for twenty-five cents," he continued, a factor that would weigh heavily when the Nikkei ultimately settled for less.

But would the BCFU have proposed a lower price to open negotiations? The union had two objectives: recognition as the bargaining agent for fishermen and establishment of a season-long price. They had to lead when it came to framing the price demand. But the failure to achieve a merger was a tough blow. Bargaining would be harder to manage and the opportunities for division were much increased.[72]

For First Nations members, there was a third goal that was never left out of their considerations: restoration of their historical dominance in the gillnet fleet as recognition of their Indigenous fishing rights. This was a political demand, which First Nations fishers, who had no right to vote, could only achieve through their own advocacy. In contrast, the Nikkei were undertaking a forceful legal strategy to win the right to vote.

Within forty-eight hours of the meeting, Rogers wrote to the *Province* protesting the continued growth of the Nikkei fleet, made possible by what he alleged was the wide-open issuance of fraudulent naturalization papers. Rogers's effort to stop the flow of new arrivals was designed to placate his membership. At the same time, he underlined the harsh reality to members who wanted to step up the call for exclusion: without unity across the Nikkei and union fleets, there was no prospect of a negotiated price.

Did the Nikkei set the price demand and then betray it? That was Watson's charge later, one he used to good effect to condemn those Nikkei who ultimately settled for less. Yet there were many reasons why the BCFU membership would have settled on a twenty-five-cent opening demand even without the Nikkei initiative. The twenty-five-cent price had been the opening price in 1899 and been maintained throughout that season, despite some deliveries above and below that level. News reports indicated twenty-five cents was already being paid on the Columbia River and on Puget Sound. The union's demand was not a major increase, but was within the range of prices paid elsewhere and in previous years with similar run expectations. What was more, Rogers later disclosed that he had urged a twenty-cent opening demand during this period, but he was overruled.

Each of the fishermen's organizations rushed to complete its preparations for bargaining as the season opening neared. Many of the Port Simpson fishers and their families had not arrived in Vancouver until June 30 and would not travel to Steveston until after the holiday weekend celebrations. They may have been in time to participate in a union membership vote on the price demand—separate votes of the BCFU's Vancouver and New Westminster locals were held that day. In Steveston, Dantai's membership endorsed the demand for twenty-five cents a fish and elected a negotiating committee. Dantai had completed its constitutional reorganization on June 29.

The canners remained silent. Their goal was always to delay announcing a price for as long as possible, ensuring that they never implied a floor price that could later be raised. Instead, they waited to assess run strength and their own internal competitive pressures, often reflected in mid-season bidding wars that drove up prices. The goal of the combine was to fix an upper limit on prices, not to fix the price for the entire season; it was expected and understood that prices would fall if that was what the markets required. What was more, posting a price cut or any price below the twenty-five-cent mark would simply assist the union organizing efforts. The united front of fishermen had splintered in the past; it was likely to do so again. Bell-Irving was doing his best to make sure of it.[73]

By Dominion Day, Steveston was bursting at the seams. Thousands of fishermen and cannery workers relaxed in the early summer sun, strolling down the boardwalks or exploring the offerings of bars, bordellos and gambling halls. Some may even have gone to church. Brass bands were a fixture, with the Salvation Army a noisy presence on Moncton Street. Thousands of gillnetters lay ready to set their nets; hundreds of canoes were dragged up on the river's banks, draped in wet cedar mats, their lengthy passages over for now.

On July 1, no one fished. The strike had begun. There were no fish in the river so the mood remained buoyant. There was time for a settlement, if one was possible, without losing income. The unions, with their price demands in hand, demanded a meeting with the canners. Another delegation met with the association on Monday, July 3, when the strike was in its third day. This time, although the canners did not release it, their decision leaked out. The price offer would be twenty cents, sources told reporters, and this maximum would be enforced by large bonds posted by individual canners that would be forfeited if anyone broke ranks. Canners reserved the right to cut the price and impose daily catch limits. Canner C.S. Windsor told reporters that some canners had been prepared to commit to twenty cents for the season but had been overruled. All sides understood that twenty cents was simply an opening position; once runs built up, successive cuts would follow quickly. This reality undoubtedly stiffened resolve on the side of the fishermen, particularly among the Dantai leadership members, who had vowed to resist a cut but had already warned Rogers they might settle below twenty-five cents.[74]

Tensions began to rise. Rumours that rifles were being moved to the Nikkei in Steveston on the stagecoach proved false (a single firearm was found).[75] But sporadic fishing, often by Nikkei fishermen, was raising alarm in BCFU ranks. Although the Nikkei, now cut off from cannery supplies, were probably fishing for spring salmon for personal consumption—a practice encouraged throughout the strike—the BCFU rank and file demanded a more solid united front. Rogers personally investigated a rumour of the Nikkei being armed, then denounced it as a "canard."[76]

The BCFU organized rallies for July 7, the end of the strike's first week, as a show of force and determination, setting that day as the deadline for a complete shutdown on the river. An afternoon mass meeting in Steveston, where MacLain was the keynote speaker, drew seven hundred fishermen; a similar evening rally in Eburne, where a ferry carried the stage across the Fraser's North Arm, drew between one hundred and three hundred. (The rickety bridge was closed for repairs.) According to news reports, about 125 fishermen formally joined the union in Eburne that day. The Steveston meeting underlined the pressures MacLain and Rogers were seeking to manage. The First Nations speaker at the Steveston rally, not named in reports, warned the white fishermen not to break ranks as they had in 1893. A Nikkei representative, likely Yamazaki, was invited to the platform to confirm Dantai's support of the twenty-five-cent demand, which he did.[77]

There was still the problem of fishing in violation of the strike. Posters suddenly appeared around Steveston declaring that "any Japanese or other fishermen selling fish at less than union rates, twenty-five cents, will be shot or have his boat stove in—the former preferred." (Boats could be "stove in" in many ways, but one particularly terrifying technique involved hurling a rock or anchor into a boat and through the planks from a passing steam tug.) Union members quickly repudiated the posters and tore them down. Whether they were a strategic provocation by the canners or the action of union members was never clear, but they had little impact on Nikkei who wished to set their nets.[78]

The *World* claimed on July 8 that nearly one thousand Nikkei boats were fishing, undoubtedly an exaggeration, but there is little doubt that significant numbers of Nikkei did go out. The official Dantai history recounts how "all the fishermen met on the dyke and started a work slowdown—no one went out to work. However, it is important to note at this time that all the [Nikkei] fishermen's food was supplied by the canneries. This calculation [for how much food each fisher was owed] was made at the end of the fishing season and deducted by the canneries from each fisherman's due remuneration—so this put the cannery owners in a very strong position." A slowdown wasn't good enough for the other fishers; a complete shutdown was required.[79]

To stop the fishing, Rogers proposed a program of picketing the length of the river, with union boats to include a Japanese interpreter where possible. Limited food fishing would be allowed. By Monday, picket boats were sweeping the fishing grounds all the way from Texada Island to Point Roberts and upriver to Mission. Boats fishing for food were instructed to fly a flag: red and white for the white boats, white for the First Nations boats and red for the Nikkei.[80] It was clear that some Nikkei fishermen were unaware of the strike, Rogers told a *World* reporter. In one case a group of a dozen Nikkei boats had their catch of one hundred fish thrown overboard, whether by the Nikkei in panic at the sight of picketers or by the picketers in righteous anger was unclear. The picketing soon became effective. Enough fish were available early in the week for some canneries to operate a few hours in the morning, but by Wednesday the shutdown was complete.

Rogers was determined to clear up any misunderstandings. On July 9 he led delegations of BCFU members, with Nikkei interpreters, from bunkhouse to bunkhouse to meet with Nikkei bosses and fishermen to impress upon them the need for solidarity. The union men "went round and visited the Japanese houses and we asked the bosses in an intelligent manner not to go out fishing," Rogers reported later.

"They said they would not. We made several visits to them. There was no other force brought to bear, only to ask the Japanese to stand by their agreement, and that when we had the matter settled we would all go fishing together." Dantai's history of these conversations recalled a tougher message. Japanese fishing would be stopped peacefully, if possible, "but if not, then force would have to be used." At least six hundred BCFU members were on the dykes to advise Nikkei fishermen, through their bosses, "that if they made any attempt to fish for less than the union rate there would be trouble and someone would get hurt."

Photographs of these marches show long lines of fishermen, clad in rough jackets and soft hats, thronging the grassy dykes along the riverside, undoubtedly a sobering sight for Nikkei preparing to fish. *The Province* reported that the delegations included men from Canada, England, Portugal, Spain, Sweden, Denmark and many nationalities, with a Japanese fisherman leading the way for translation. The Nikkei were respectful but unintimidated. Many were practising martial arts in the fields behind the canneries. But the union left no room for misunderstanding. "They warned the Jap boss not to allow his men to fish," the *Province* reported. The strike remained solid.[81]

The canners took immediate steps to counteract the picketing, wiring newly appointed Attorney General D.M. Eberts on July 10 that "riots and damage to property likely to result unless immediate and ample police protection afforded to men desirous of pursing their lawful calling; armed strikers parading Steveston." Posters, using exactly the same language that had proved effective in 1893, went up around Steveston over Duncan's name offering $100 for information leading to the arrest and conviction of anyone cutting nets, intimidating strikebreakers or threatening violence.

Chief Constable R.B. Lister, who visited Steveston Tuesday night after asking Victoria to send a batch of badges for special constables, saw nothing to cause alarm, a view reinforced by news reports. "All quiet here at present," Lister telegraphed Eberts. Lister believed that most fishermen would return to the grounds had they not been under the spell of "labour agitators" like MacLain and union president J.L. Anderson. He arranged for four cannery tugs to be available for patrol and took steps to secure special constables to crew them.[82]

Confident he could end the strike by decapitating the union, Lister arranged for Colin Campbell, one of his subordinates, to contrive the arrest of Anderson as he picketed in English Bay. The complaint against Anderson, written up by a young First Nations fisher under the direction of his cannery boss, was summarily thrown out of court. Charges against Anderson were dismissed. Each of the high-profile arrests of union leaders—first Anderson and then Rogers— was timed to clear the way for a return to work, especially by the Nikkei. This time, the tactic failed; the arrest handed the union a propaganda victory. The close cooperation among employers was further illuminated when MacLain was fired by the CPR. He laughed it off—just more time to organize the strike.[83]

Lister's meetings with the canners were a matter of public knowledge, reported in the daily papers along with strike-related court proceedings. Bell-Irving's diary and the minutes of the salmon canners show how closely the owner of ABC Packing directed events, maintaining constant contact with other canners, police, the Japanese consulate and others. In Vancouver's compact downtown core, the canners' offices, the union's office, the major daily newsrooms and the bars of a score of hotels offered countless convenient places to scheme, gossip and negotiate. A mass meeting of the fishermen passed a lengthy resolution designed to reassure the Nikkei and the people of Vancouver, who were receiving lengthy daily updates on strike developments in the city's three major dailies. The threatening posters placed around Steveston were part of a campaign to provoke resentment of the fishermen, the union men said: "Be it resolved that this union views with regret and alarm the action of the canners in arresting Captain Anderson, and would urge all fishermen to refrain from all intimidation and violence, but to use all lawful means to keep men from fishing under the price." In response to Anderson's arrest, the labour movement planned a "monster" march and rally for the next Saturday, July 14.[84]

Not content with paying the salaries of police constables, the canners now turned to the Japanese consul to communicate with his fellow countrymen. "It appears that those who are engaged in fair fishing face increasing interference and threats of violence," wrote Consul General Shimuzu. "The canners' cooperative has used a steamboat, ordered in police and will see that safe fishing is guaranteed. Honest fishermen will be protected at all costs. Please take comfort in this protection and go out and fish industriously." Japanese fishermen could defend themselves, he concluded, but "must never strike out at others." In the event of a confrontation, the Nikkei were urged to write down the details and report to the cannery association to receive a reward. In the event of injury or loss of gear, "the damages will be paid by the association." Japanese immigration to BC had stopped, he told *The World*, but he was unable to give details.[85]

The BCFU had its own problems. Some of its members, particularly in the New Westminster local, were also on the fishing grounds, complaining that the twenty-five-cent demand was too high. This local, dominated by white fishermen who worked nearly year-round on spring, sockeye and chum salmon runs, was militantly anti-Asiatic.

To underline the unity of the fishermen, Dantai leaders including Yamazaki were brought to a union meeting on July 10 to repeat once more Dantai's determination to achieve twenty-five cents. This they did, but the Nikkei union leaders were blunt about pressures they faced in a private meeting with the BCFU. After more than a week on strike, their members were starving.

Yamazaki and Dantai president Iwakichi Shimamura reminded the BCFU leaders that:

> there are four thousand Japanese here engaged in the fishing industry. At the start of the fishing season, this class of people came here like an arrowhead, planning to fish ... When this white fishermen's strike happened, we felt from our perspective we needed to show sympathy with the white fishermen. Because of this, our food payments were cut by the canneries. And so because of this we cannot strike. If the strike is to continue, for its duration, we would like to be supplied by the white union the amount of money required to cover our food expenses. If this cannot be done, we will go out fishing for less than twenty-five cents per fish. Otherwise we cannot deal with our current emergency.

The two unions agreed on the spot to permit food fisheries with a daily catch limit of three hundred sockeye for each organization. The BCFU also took steps to provide much larger food supplies to Steveston strikers, hundreds of whom were headed to Vancouver July 14 for the downtown march and rally. Before they adjourned, the BCFU leaders selected a new negotiating committee of fishermen only; Rogers, Watson and MacLain were excluded to answer the charge that the fishermen were being manipulated by outside agitators.[86]

The pressure on the Dantai leadership must have been extreme. In Steveston, they were seeking to restrain thousands of frustrated, hungry men. The bosses themselves were required to provide whatever food they could on their own account, hoping to recover it from later earnings. But when would those earnings begin? If the BCFU wanted to avoid a collapse by Dantai, they would have to find a way to deliver food to Steveston. This would amount to a direct test of labour solidarity: in a city consumed by anti-Asiatic rhetoric, would average people answer this appeal for help?

Once again the sidewalks of downtown Vancouver were crowded by spectators, this time in sunny weather, to watch a march. In Steveston, some eighteen hundred BCFU supporters had rallied and marched once more to the Nikkei bunkhouses, where "cheers and tigers were given for Japanese who promised to stand by the white union." According to one estimate, the Nikkei fishers and boat pullers now numbered five thousand. Despite the promise of police protection, "the Japs have racked their nets and taken up their boats and say they will not fish until a general settlement is arrived at."

Between five hundred and one thousand fishermen circled the business district on July 14—"whites, Indians and negroes but no Japanese," according to the *Province*— leaving no doubt the strike remained solid. Soon after lunch, the long column of fishermen and supporters headed off, three abreast, led by Lax Kw'alaams musicians and bolstered by the addition of two hundred new members who were said to have joined the union in the previous twenty-four hours. "The Port Simpson band was discoursing all kinds of marches and ragtime music at the head of a long line," the *Province* reported, "with their drum major in a uniform that would put a German admiral out of business, [who] swung his baton and blew his whistle in a more artistic way." Banners reading *25 Cents or No Fish* were scattered through the ranks. Union leaders, including Captain Anderson, rode in horse-drawn carriages near the head of the procession.[87]

Once the strikers had gathered in front of the courthouse, the speeches got underway. The speakers represented the entire spectrum of strike leadership except the Nikkei. J.H. Watson, the first up to speak at the courthouse, declared the main goal to be recognition of the union. A friendly compromise was in order, he said, and the canners would "find the fishermen not unreasonable if they treated the fishermen like men."[88]

But the subsequent speakers took a very different direction, aiming all their rhetorical fire at the Japanese the Steveston fishermen had been cheering the night before. United Socialist Labour Party leader Ernest Burns said a defeat for the fishermen would mean even larger numbers of Nikkei on the grounds and price cuts to fifteen or even ten cents later in the season. Worse, he warned, was the possibility that Japanese fishermen would move to other industries in the province and undercut their wages as well. This was an issue, he declared, for all "white" labour.

Then it was Chief George Kelly's turn, in a speech that was remarked on by everyone who heard it. Although Kelly's precise role was never spelled out, he was the undoubted leader of the First Nations fleet in the eyes of outsiders. Nikkei historians of the dispute saw him as leader both of the Lax Kw'alaams and other First Nations, participating in the bargaining through the BCFU. Kelly emphasized that he himself was a voter—in other words, not an Indian prohibited from voting under BC law, probably the result of his mother marrying a non-Indigenous man. He had no use for Chinese or Japanese, he said to loud applause, and would never vote for a Japanese to go to Parliament. If any Japanese dared to fish, Kelly boasted, he would deal with them—he had the strength of five or six men. Police officer Colin Campbell, who was observing from the crowd, recalled the speech weeks later as "especially provocative with regard to the Japanese."[89]

MacLain wound up the proceedings with a threat to organize a British boycott of canned salmon if no agreement was achieved. The tireless Nelson's Cornet Band wound up the day with yet another concert in a downtown park. That night, Yamazaki was again called to the union hall to recommit Dantai's support for the strike, which he did. This must have been a strained conversation. Despite the speeches, the union was taking practical steps to respond to the Nikkei fishermen's plight. The collection that day totalled $225, and union-friendly businesses were canvassed for food to be distributed in Steveston. Food began to flow to Steveston, proof that solidarity was stronger than racial animosity among Vancouver workers. Nonetheless, the canners confidently predicted the fleet, Nikkei and white, would return to work under Lister's protection when the gun sounded Sunday night to inaugurate that week's harvest. The salmon strike, they said, already the longest in the industry's history and the largest in BC's history, would be over by July 15.[90]

The union show of force in Vancouver sparked apocalyptic media warnings of violent clashes to come when fishing resumed Sunday evening, including "armed conflict" likely to end in "loss of life."[91] When fishing opened Sunday night, picketing was intensive. News reports suggested a few strikebreakers were present in every section of the fleet. A pair of fishermen, one white and Nikkei, were confronted off Sand Heads light; pickets took them in tow and headed back to Steveston. When a cannery tug arrived to give chase, the

union men headed for shallow water and the tug, manoeuvring frantically to head them off, then cut the strikebreakers'
boat in two and threw them into the water. Both union men
and the cannery's enforcers cooperated to affect a rescue
before the picketers disappeared into the gloom.

Elsewhere that night, MacLain was spotted in a picket
boat that confronted officials of the Albion cannery who had
set a net. They claimed to be testing special equipment on
SS *Albion* that was intended to allow the tug to pass over nets
without cutting them. According to the indignant account
of the *Albion*'s skipper, MacLain's men, led by a Nikkei fisherman, had attacked the men in the company's gillnet skiff.[92]

Food now began flowing into Steveston from sympathizers in Vancouver. A commissary set up in Steveston
began feeding several hundred strikers daily. Union bakers
sent contributions of bread, and the food fishery was working
more smoothly. MacLain and Rogers began planning a tour
of labour-friendly communities, starting with the Nanaimo
coal miners, to increase their support. There was little time
to lose; rumours were growing that the sockeye runs were
building up in the Strait of Georgia, although Boundary Bay
salmon traps reported mostly spring salmon in their pens.[93]

The strikers' pressure was proving effective. All day
Tuesday and again on Wednesday, the canners' committee
met with a delegation of fishermen under the supervision
of Dominion Labour Commissioner E.P. Bremner, who was
trying to find middle ground. Initially, the canners remained
inflexible on the twenty-cent offer, along with the right to cut
prices as they saw fit. As the talks wore on, they proposed
a twenty-cent maximum and a fifteen-cent minimum, but
the fishermen held firm. There were rumours, Rogers told
reporters, that the militia might be called out. In Steveston,
a Dantai membership meeting at the new hospital debated

whether to accept the twenty-cent offer. The offer was reasonable, the fishing bosses argued, and the key BCFU leaders—no doubt a reference to Watson, MacLain and Rogers—were not even fishermen. The Nikkei membership began to shift: there should be no settlement below twenty cents, they agreed, but that season-long flat price was still not on offer. The strike would continue.[94]

The Nikkei were not the only fishermen beginning to look for a settlement. In New Westminster, where anti-Japanese settlement was most intense, the union membership was also arguing for a twenty-cent season-long price. Significant numbers of fishermen set their nets July 17—some of them Nikkei in Steveston and others the white fishermen of New Westminster. Other white fishermen broke ranks briefly on July 19 at the North Arm of the Fraser, where the village of Eburne had grown up at the ferry crossing.

There is little doubt the canners became aware of these developments the moment they occurred, and news of the debates in Steveston and New Westminster quickly found their way into Vancouver's newspapers, which were fiercely competitive. The BCFU was equally quick to make note of apparent breaches in the canners' front. When Captain Anderson phoned in reports that Kamekichi Ohki, vice-president of Dantai, had invested $15,000 in the Lighthouse Cannery and was prepared to push for a twenty-five-cent settlement, the *Province* quickly printed the news.

The next day, however, the paper told readers that the Lighthouse management had declared the report an "absolute falsehood" and condemned Anderson as "a purveyor of unreliable reports." Nonetheless, it was a fact that Ohki was provided an office by the cannery from which he conducted Dantai business and, according to some reports, helped manage production. Whether or not Anderson's report had any basis in reality, the *Province*'s reversal probably also signalled a determined effort by the canners to curb sympathetic coverage for the strikers, who clearly enjoyed broad support in the city's working class. By the end of the week, the paper was denouncing MacLain as a demagogue and Rogers's leadership as the "dictatorship of a blatant and injudicious blatherskite."[95]

It was against this backdrop—and the opening of the legislature for the first time since the June election—that the BCFU leadership met Friday evening in Vancouver. The negotiations that week had produced a feeling of optimism; the breaches in the strikers' front had been short-term and quickly brought under control. The canners had raised their minimum price offer to eighteen cents. The union negotiators had countered with a settlement framework of twenty cents a fish with one month's notice of any price reduction, no discrimination against union members and identical delivery limits for cannery and independent fishermen. This position only prevailed in the fishermen's bargaining committee by a narrow 3–2 vote, indicating how close a settlement was.

But the canners refused to close the gap, insisting that agreement would come only if the fishermen's committee accepted on the spot, without a vote of the membership. The union delegation waited until 10 p.m. to receive reports from various locals on the river, as well as the Nikkei and First Nations fleets. A split emerged. The New Westminster and Nikkei fishermen were prepared to move to twenty cents, but the Steveston and North Arm fleets were determined to hold firm for twenty-five cents. The talks broke down.[96]

The BCFU leadership faced some difficult calculations. So far, unity with the Nikkei fleet was firm and the canners' withdrawal of food had been overcome by a steady flow of groceries from Vancouver. Precisely how much food arrived is unclear, but even wholesalers contributed: bags of potatoes, rice and vegetables made their way to Steveston to supplement the food fishery. There was little doubt public opinion was on the side of the union and understood the need to support the Nikkei fishermen. Some smaller sections of the union fleet were faltering, but the membership in Steveston, the heart of the fishery, had actually grown since the strike began. The sockeye were not yet running; the point of maximum pressure was still to come.

The rumours of a militia intervention must have provoked intense speculation. Soldiers might be of use to breach a picket line outside a mine, for example, but what could they do against pickets who ranged over a vast stretch of the Strait of Georgia, especially at night? Despite the fiery rhetoric at the previous weekend's Vancouver rally, the BCFU remained in close contact with the Dantai leadership and First Nations chiefs. The negotiating committee that was gathered in Vancouver debated late into the evening about its next moves. With the strike nearly three weeks old, they decided to stand firm.

Did the canners really want a settlement? Bell-Irving certainly did not. Very few canners would support even the implicit recognition of the union provided by a formal price agreement. Others may have been encouraged by the week's fishing incidents to believe the strike was about to collapse. The propaganda battle continued in the papers, with an ad hoc bankers' committee concluding unanimously that the canners would lose money even at twenty cents. (Bell-Irving needed no instruction in media strategy.) Canners mused to reporters about shutting down for the entire season, even though square-riggers chartered to take the pack to England were already paid for and waiting in Steveston for cargo.

Whatever their internal debates, the canners' unity—
"Unity" was their cable and telegram address—proved solid.
Although canner C.S. Windsor had supported recognition
of the union, the majority focused on breaking the strike.
Like the fishermen, they were aware the sockeye had not yet
reached the Strait of Georgia. The demand that the fishermen
ratify the settlement without consulting the membership—
when the settlement price offered was five cents below the
last membership mandate—was no doubt intended more for
public relations purposes than for an attempt at a settlement.
Had the BCFU leaders accepted, the membership would have
been outraged. But the offer had the advantage of showing
the canners as willing to compromise.[97]

The canners had no time to wait for a fishermen's vote
for another reason: they were about to execute a careful plan
to provoke violence on the river. The evening after union
fishermen rejected the canners' ultimatum, two gillnetters
set out from Bell-Irving's Phoenix cannery in Steveston
protected by three cannery tugs carrying ten special constables. Lister, who cannot have been ignorant about the foray,
wrote later that the goal was "evidently to test the attitude
of the strikers." Picket boats were quickly on the scene and,
despite the police presence, one of the non-union boats was
captured and towed to a Steveston wharf where a crowd
quickly gathered. George Brown was the net man on the
boat, and Arthur Kipps was the boat puller. One of the two—
there was confusion about which one—was hauled before
the crowd and forced up on a wooden box to be ridiculed.

There were nine or ten boats on the river that night,
Rogers said later. In testimony to a special committee of the
legislature struck to investigate, Rogers said he believed a
man named Munro was in charge of the canners' forces:

Word was brought to me that one of the canners intended to send out some men fishing, and see if the strikers' patrol boats would induce these men to take up their nets and not go fishing, and that they would have a couple of tugboats there with special police on them, but the police were only to make a showing and not to arrest anyone, and if they got this thing up they would have an opportunity of calling out the militia ...

I wanted to test if these people had the power to call out the militia on such a trifling question as that. I went out in one of the boats, and we asked this man to take up his net and not fish, and not betray himself as a traitor to the white men and sell himself for a few paltry dollars. The man simply folded his arms, and says, "All right."

This was not the outcome the police had expected. Rogers continued:

In the meantime, the tugboat *Winnifred* came alongside with this man Munro in it, and he says to the man Kipp, "Are you in danger?" Kipp says, "No; I am not in any danger." Munro says, "Do you want any help?" Kipp says, "No. There's some of these men in my boat, but I am not in any real danger." Munro says to the special policemen, "Arrest these men and protect this man." The special police did not seem to make any effort to board the boat.

The strikers quickly towed the strikebreakers to shore. Either Kipp—or was it Brown?—was put ashore and dragged up on a box, where the strikers subjected him to jeers and insults. Shaking with fear, the would-be strikebreaker was held on the box while some strikers debated throwing him in the river. This, too, was likely not what he had expected when he agreed to play a role for the police. Rogers said later:

> I asked the man if he did not think he was doing a very foolish thing, and asked him if he did not think himself very low to sell himself for a few dollars. He gave us no answer, and the men called him a scab. We told him we didn't want him to go fishing anymore, and I gave him a little shove off the box, and when he got down somebody did strike him; but even a case like that didn't call for the militia, and there was a special constable on the wharf at the time if he wished to make any arrests. That was the case of intimidation brought against me. I wanted to see if they had the power to call out the militia; and, of course, they did call them out, whether they had the power or not.[98]

Although Rogers admitted pushing the man off the box, there was conflicting evidence as to what happened next. Was the scab shoved and kicked, bruised all over, as some said? It was dark. Fisherman Hugh Campbell told the committee that Rogers had jumped up on the box and said, "Boys, if you do anything, don't do anything to violate the law; it will be pretty bad for us and hurt our cause."[99]

No firearms had been seen on either side, no injury was done to the strikebreakers beyond some insults and some shoving. Nonetheless, two days later police arrested Rogers and bundled him into a stagecoach to be taken to Vancouver. The canners had sought to provoke an incident, and Rogers was keen to be provoked. The result was much less compelling than Bell-Irving's canners had hoped, but they would make do.

Rogers's challenge to the strikebreaker—"to not betray himself as a traitor to the white men"—is the only example in the history of the 1900 and 1901 strikes of the BCFU leader making a direct racial appeal. The files of Ottawa's Department of Marine and Fisheries contained many telegrams from Rogers protesting the wholesale and fraudulent naturalization of Nikkei fishermen, all in the name of the BCFU, but racist rhetoric was never the basis of Rogers's advocacy. As a member of the United Socialist Labour Party, Rogers must be considered a sympathizer, at the very least, of the Asiatic exclusion views of men like Socialist leader Ernest Burns, a featured speaker at the previous weekend's rally. Would Bell-Irving's provocation have fizzled out so decisively if the strikebreakers seized by the picketers had been defiant Nikkei fishermen? Some reports indicated another gillnetter out that night had both Nikkei and white men aboard.

Rogers's account of this incident, transcribed by a legislature stenographer, is one of only two occasions when we hear Rogers in his own words. He was clearly downplaying the significance of those events, but they marked a turning point in the strike, perhaps the point at which the possibility of cooperation across race lines became impossible. Rogers's test provided the canners a pretext, whether he realized it or not, for a decisive move to break the fragile united front the BCFU had crafted with Dantai despite the clear animosity of union members, including members of the First Nations locals. All the appeals for unity, the joint picketing and the food relief would be rendered worthless when that moment came.

In Vancouver, the canners had allowed negotiations to break down. Henry Bell-Irving executed his strategy with careful efficiency. Within minutes of the incident in Steveston, Dr. Duncan Bell-Irving and William Farrell of the canners' executive committee had wired Victoria to complain that the special constables were useless; they "saw riot and unlawful acts by the strikers without attempting to offer aid." The canners' Pinkerton detective, who by remarkable coincidence had been present on the dock, had witnessed these outrages.[100]

The confrontation on the Fraser, despite its lack of overt violence and comedic overtones, had worked: everyone played their part acceptably. Bell-Irving's efforts to justify calling out the militia were unfolding as planned.[101] The call for military force was endorsed by a Board of Trade meeting on Saturday afternoon. Only twenty of two hundred members could participate on such short notice—most of them canners. Not surprisingly, a motion presented by Henry Bell-Irving declared a "state of lawlessness" on the river that required immediate provincial action "for the full protection of life and property." Telegrams clattered off the wires in Ottawa and Victoria, demanding deployment of the fisheries patrol vessel *Quadra* by one government and the militia by the other. In Victoria, Premier James Dunsmuir was relaxing in his hilltop mansion. The legislature had finally reconvened just two days before with the Speech from the Throne. His government made no reply to the weekend appeals.[102]

The canners moved Saturday to secure Dantai's support, refining their "final" position in a secret meeting with a Nikkei delegation. Who made up that delegation is not recorded in the Fraser River Canners' Association minute book, but the discussion was brief. The canners now offered to pay twenty cents for the first six hundred fish each week and fifteen cents for any over that figure. This was a decisive shift designed to win the support of the one group that could end the strike or prolong it: the members of Dantai. The negotiations in Vancouver ended Saturday at 5:30 p.m., just under twenty-four hours before fishing was to begin for the week. The Nikkei leaders quickly communicated the offer to their members, as did the canners, posting the terms along Steveston dykes by Sunday morning.

The sudden offer must have been anticipated by the union leadership but nonetheless struck like a bombshell. The Saturday newspapers had been frantic with warnings about impending violence, but violence would only result if there were a concerted attempt to fish in defiance of the strike. That would take an organized effort by the Nikkei fleet, but as far as anyone knew, the Nikkei fleet had not settled. The BCFU leadership learned of Dantai's settlement by word of mouth. By Saturday evening, the word was out: the Nikkei leadership had accepted the new offer. This time, there had been no meeting by Dantai with the BCFU or First Nations.

The Steveston fishermen were demoralized and disoriented. The previous morning, the police had played their appointed role in Bell-Irving's strategy by arresting Rogers on charges of intimidation as a result of the Friday night confrontation. He was bundled into a stagecoach and shipped to a Vancouver jail cell. But just as quickly, Rogers returned, his charges dismissed for lack of evidence. Faced with the Nikkei leadership's recommendation, the BCFU leaders decided to take a vote of their own.[103]

Dantai leaders called a massive rally of their members to ratify the settlement. Between thirty-five hundred and four thousand filled the fields behind the canneries to hear rousing speeches from Yamazaki and the bosses. Aware that several hundred of his members might sympathize with the union and hundreds more might be afraid of violence, he emphasized the authorities' promise to provide appropriate protection. Rintaro Hayashi, who became one of the most important leaders of Dantai for the next thirty years, wrote later that "when the speeches ended and the countermeasures were announced, three thousand Japanese gave the imperial banzai three times. They then formed a magnificent rank and paraded from one end of the Steveston fishing village to the other." Observers declared that the gathering was the largest in the town's history. The vote, by show of hands, was unanimous. The Japanese—termed the "little brown men" by the *Province*—then marched behind a rising sun flag to their bunkhouses, their shouts of "Banzai!" still echoing across the dykes. A counter-demonstration by union fishermen mustered only five hundred to six hundred men.[104]

The Nikkei vote, however, was not as united as the demonstration suggested. Dissidents had already been dealt with behind the scenes through Dantai's own quasi-judicial processes, as Teiji Kobayashi, author of Dantai's history, later recalled:

> The fishers' Dantai ... had their own court which could impose banishments and fines. In the midst of this trouble the following was spoken against the idea of going out fishing: "We existed between life and death during the Sino-Japanese War and managed to get through. We came all the way to this country and now don't want to enter the same kind of danger again." And using this as guidance about forty people made a similar proposal. Immediately some of their members were exiled from Steveston, and others were fined—this drew great argument. Looking back this seems excessive, but at the time it was very important to keep order and organization. If a problem had occurred at this point, though not welcome, great bloodshed—like a rain of blood—would have been unavoidable. There were many reckless daredevils on both sides, so there was no other way to stop this from going to its natural conclusion.[105]

Now it was the BCFU's turn. In an open field behind the Steveston Opera House, more than fifteen hundred gathered to hear addresses from Rogers and MacLain. Rogers chaired the meeting. MacLain had rushed back from a solidarity and fundraising tour of communities around the southern Strait of Georgia, including New Westminster and Nanaimo. A key attraction was the Port Simpson Nelson's Cornet Band, which won favourable reviews at every stop. The first speaker was E.P. Bremner, the federal mediator who had been seeking a compromise. The price proposed by the canners was their final offer, he warned, and their costs exceedingly high. The fishermen listened closely. Then it was MacLain's turn to speak, and then Burns's. This time, there was little appeal to emotion, just a careful assessment of the opposing forces. Neither dared make a recommendation.

Then the fishermen were separated from the rest and wrote their preferred settlement price—twenty-five cents, twenty-two cents or twenty cents—on a blank piece of paper. As hundreds watched, fishermen of all races and nationalities lined up to vote, dropping their ballots in a covered hat placed on a table in the open field. "Among the loitering crowds at one side," reported the *World*, "was a collection of what appeared to be half the Indian population of British Columbia. They sat on the grass in the sun and talked among themselves. Their women were dressed in all the gaudy colours of the rainbow. There were all the nationalities ranging between the Indians and the whites—from the Mexican with hair hanging down his back to Chileans and Kanakas."

Four men, including First Nations fishers, acted as scrutineers; two reporters were asked to supervise the count. A total of 492 votes were in favour of twenty-five cents, 15 for twenty-two cents and 27 for twenty cents. Of the 541 ballots cast, 7 were spoiled. The cheering that erupted at the announcement of the vote "fairly woke the town." The strike would continue. MacLain and other strikers aboard the steamer *Starling* found few boats on the river that night. Rogers professed himself confident few would venture out at dawn, either. If they did, one thousand white fishermen would meet them.[106]

The Nikkei fishermen had prepared their boats for fishing on the morning tide, but dawn brought new delays. Their bosses, suddenly cautious, then held them back: the protection offered by the canners just thirty-six hours before was nowhere to be seen. The Nikkei were uncertain. Their determination to settle had been strongly influenced by direct commitments of protection against union pickets. Yamazaki, who had organized his own violent attacks on strikebreakers on the Skeena, knew how dangerous it would be to send the fleet out to the fickle, windswept waters of the Fraser without substantial police support.[107]

Probably aware the canners were mobilizing the militia, the Dantai leadership issued an urgent notice that fishing would not begin until the next day. In effect, the strike continued. In an effort to maintain their momentum and to dispel any claim they were intimidated, the Nikkei leaders organized another afternoon rally "to demonstrate our strength." Their appeal read: "Everyone's presence is requested, except cooks and women." The Nikkei fishermen dutifully demonstrated a second time.[108] A second night passed without fishing. At dawn, dramatic news spread down the dykes and docks: soldiers were disembarking on the public wharf from the steamer *Comox*.

CHAPTER 6

SOLDIERS OF THE QUEEN

Henry Bell-Irving had spent all day Monday in a state of barely controlled rage. With the fishermen finally split and victory within his grasp, he was unable to mobilize support from his own business and political allies. The Sunday settlement with the Nikkei had been linked to a guarantee of protection against violent attacks from union pickets. The Nikkei fleet was now poised to sail, but appeals to Ottawa and Victoria to deploy the militia had been received in silence.

The demands of canners, dominated by Conservative supporters, were of little interest to Liberal Prime Minister Wilfrid Laurier in Ottawa. Laurier no doubt felt he had spent enough time that year seeking to calm the province's roiled political waters. BC's new lieutenant governor, Henri Joly de Lotbiniere, was still cleaning up the chaos left by Thomas

McInnes. Let the locals sort out their own affairs, the prime minister decided. Ottawa made no response to demands that the fisheries vessel *Quadra* be deployed in support of the canners.

Nor was newly elected Premier James Dunsmuir keen to come to the rescue. Although his father Robert had used the militia to suppress at least two miners' strikes, Dunsmuir's unsteady political coalition in Victoria could not afford to turn the initiative over to labour-friendly members of the legislature, whose voters were demanding expulsion of Asiatics, not support for their use as strikebreakers. Indeed, the Throne Speech delivered just days earlier had promised strong government pressure in Ottawa to curb the "the alarming increase of the Japanese population."[109]

Attorney General David Eberts, a fellow Conservative, had done his best to support Bell-Irving throughout the dispute. It was Eberts who hired three special constables recommended by the canners at the beginning of the season, and it was Eberts who hounded Chief Constable R.B. Lister for news of the dispute and ordered him to be prepared to read the Riot Act as early as July 11. Lister seemed unable to appreciate the urgency of the situation, stubbornly reporting general calm along Steveston's docks. Dr. Duncan Bell-Irving told Eberts July 20 that the special constables were "unable to cope with the situation" and "useless." A telegram the next day went further, declaring the "utterly useless" police were "treated with absolute contempt." Only the militia would do, he fumed.

Even after Rogers humiliated Bell-Irving's strikebreakers on the Steveston dock, Lister reported July 21 that he had seen "no disturbance" in Steveston apart from that minor confrontation. There was no reason for great alarm, although the strikers were "no doubt all of the lowest grade of society."

Controlling four hundred to five hundred picketers across hundreds of square kilometres of ocean was an impossibility, Lister wrote. In any case, he had offered protection when requested, "which is only twice." This was not information that supported the costly deployment of armed militiamen.

Eberts's anger blew into fury when Lister reported from his office in Vancouver that he had authorized a deputy to read the Riot Act on Sunday if pickets interfered with fishermen headed for the grounds. "Why are you in Vancouver?" the attorney general demanded. He had been handling Rogers's arrest, Lister replied. In a flurry of telegrams, Eberts first ordered Lister to hire additional steamers and to add even more constables. He then sacked Lister and replaced him with W.H. Bullock-Webster of Nelson, someone more in line with the canners' needs. Despite these measures, though, Eberts was unable to convince Dunsmuir to take stronger action.[110]

Thwarted in Ottawa and Victoria, Bell-Irving was forced to resort to an extraordinary measure: a little-known clause in the Militia and Defence Act that allowed municipal officials to call out the militia. Bell-Irving foresaw insurrection in Steveston; if the officials of the tiny municipality of Richmond agreed, they could call out armed forces with a simple requisition signed by three local justices of the peace.[111]

The canners later pronounced themselves at least as worried about the safety of white fishermen as they were desirous of ensuring the Nikkei could fish unmolested. Their concerns were reasonable, but this was a confrontation they had worked night and day to provoke. BCFU members had made violent, racist threats to attentive reporters, and Rogers had expressed his own concern that First Nations fishers would react with violence if the Nikkei attempted to break the strike. The canners had been quick to circulate rumours that union pickets had been seen with rifles; newspaper reports made the same charge against the Nikkei fishermen. Now, thanks to the settlement with Dantai, several thousand Nikkei men—tough, recent arrivals short of food, without income, familiar with martial arts, some only in their twenties—were ready to fish. There was every reason to expect violent confrontations on the Fraser.

It fell to Bell-Irving's Pinkertons to round up the necessary signatures to declare some form of martial law. A man named Donahue, the canners' undercover Pinkerton detective, acted as courier, shuttling the requisition first from the local justices of the peace in Steveston to their counterpart near the North Arm and finally to Lieutenant Colonel C.A. Worsnop, who had been advised to remain on standby in Vancouver. Donahue, who the *Province* later noted "has many years' experience in labour troubles," made his first stop at the Malcolm and Windsor Cannery in Steveston, where he met Lister and two justices of the peace. One was Edward J. Hunt, a Steveston storekeeper and former cannery owner; the second was Robert Whiteside, a foreman at Pacific Coast cannery. Not surprisingly, both were prepared to sign the requisition without even inquiring as to the legal grounds. Donahue's next stop was on the North Arm where Justice of the Peace R.B. Wilkinson, owner of the Dinsmore Cannery, added his name. Wilkinson, a reeve of Richmond, the nearest municipality, was the only person involved in the requisition who held an elected office of any sort.

Worsnop, warned as early as 9 p.m. that the document was on its way, had ordered the steamer *Comox* to raise steam and stand by to sail from the CPR wharf at the north foot of Burrard. The moment the requisition was in his hands at 11:45 p.m., he ordered trumpeters to rouse his soldiers, most of whom were probably sleeping in their uniforms. The buglers circled around the West End mansions on a streetcar, blowing the call to arms. Members of the public once again came out to see the DCOR head off to battle. This time those gathered on the wharf sent off the soldiers with jeers and insults.

Four companies had answered the call and were handed their rifles, ten rounds of ball cartridge and twenty rounds in reserve—"ball ammunition ... as deadly as any supplied to soldiers in South Africa." Their orders were "shoot to kill." Morale on the *Comox* was low. "It was a miserable affair," one regimental history recorded. "There had been no violence and many considered the military had no right to be there at all." Defending the Empire was one thing; defending canners against union fishermen something else altogether. The *Comox* headed through First Narrows just after 3 a.m. and was alongside the Steveston dock three hours later.[112]

Worsnop quickly ordered his men ashore, where they pitched their tents in the grassy field behind the Malcolm and Windsor Cannery. Sentries patrolled the perimeter, but the mood soon eased. Rifles were propped up in threes and fours around the militia campground. The sun drummed down with almost South African intensity. A supply of wide-brimmed hats was purchased to replace the regular pillbox hats and the militiamen cut tin stars from cannery scraps to pin back the brims. As wars went, this one was tolerable; the main risk was heatstroke.[113]

The Nikkei, who had been waiting for proof of protection as well as a favourable tide, began trickling away from the docks at about 8:30, and by 10 a.m. hundreds had set their nets. The gaff-rigged sails of their skiffs, with rising sun flags fluttering from the mastheads, made a dramatic impact on observers standing on the Steveston dyke. Among the white fishermen there was a renewed sense of despair. "There are four thousand Japs, two hundred militia, one hundred police and the canners," wrote the *Province*, "against seven hundred British fishermen and a few Canadian Indians."[114] A combination of quick organizing and good luck soon put the union back on its feet. Despite the break of the majority of the Nikkei fleet, between one-third and half of the boats remained tied up—boats that were crewed by white and Indigenous fishers as well as several hundred of what Rogers termed "old-time Japs."

Rogers had been released less than twenty-four hours after his arrest. Two eyewitnesses who claimed to have seen Rogers lead the pickets against Brown were now unwilling or unable to repeat the statements they had made to Lister before Rogers's arrest. The larger objective—breaking the strike—seemed to have been accomplished. Yet Rogers predicted a prolonged struggle in an interview outside the prison with a waiting *Vancouver Daily World* reporter. Six hundred of the Japanese fishermen remained loyal to the strike, he claimed. He blamed the treachery of Kamekichi Ohki, a leading contractor, for the majority's decision to fish.

"The natives swear revenge on the Japs and threaten to kill them," said Rogers. The *Daily World* reported that "it had been the hardest task [Rogers] ever had to keep them from committing bloodshed." It was the canners, particularly Bell-Irving, who had caused the strike by their refusal to recognize the union, Rogers said. He underlined this message at every opportunity: union recognition, not just a minimum price, was key to settlement. He then rushed back to Steveston, a dusty, morning-long trip by stagecoach, where he quickly called union supporters to a meeting.[115]

The strikers on the Fraser were quick to rally. It was twenty-five cents or nothing, they declared, then marched around Steveston, hundreds strong, a huge Union Jack leading the way. The parade swirled down the dykes and around the bell tents and sentries of the two hundred armed militiamen, including Vancouver workers who had never expected their military service to include strikebreaking. Once again, members of the Duke of Connaught's Own Rifles heard choruses of "Soldiers of the Queen," the British Army's regimental marching tune, this time sung with biting sarcasm: "When we say we've always won, and they ask us how it's done, we'll proudly say, 'We're soldiers of the Queen.'" The jeering strikers had dubbed the Dukes "the Sockeye Fusiliers." Bell-Irving, observing the chaotic scene, urged Worsnop to read the Riot Act. The veteran of Batoche wisely refused.

Canners with a large contingent of Nikkei fishers began to resume limited production; others, reliant on white or Indigenous fishers, remained shut down. By evening, it was clear the BCFU had taken a body blow, but the strike had not collapsed. The fishing did not go smoothly. Many of the Nikkei men, with little or no experience in the fishery, struggled to make decent catches. Others, probably the "old-timers," were said to be dismayed that the strike had not been settled, claiming their leaders had falsely indicated all fishermen would be returning to work. As vice-president of the JFBA and a manager at the Lighthouse Cannery, Ohki was widely blamed for this treachery, for which he allegedly accepted a personal $1,500 payment from the canners.

The role of the fish bosses in the resolution of the strike would remain controversial. The JFBA constitution spelled out their control over the fishermen. Each fisher paid 1.5 percent of his wages directly to his boss, who calculated the deductions before releasing his pay. Nikkei fishers were tied both to the boss and to his cannery, and were required to notify him if they wanted to fish for someone else. This dependency was entrenched in the JFBA constitution, making it a community society rather than a union. The twenty to fifty Nikkei bosses made good use of their leadership in Dantai, missing no opportunity to disparage the BCFU leaders and their insistence on twenty-five cents. Their efforts paid off for the canners when most of the Nikkei fleet, isolated by language and racism, accepted the twenty-cent offer.[116]

Maintaining some support in the Nikkei fleet was not the only challenge faced by Rogers, now largely leading the Steveston struggle on his own while MacLain resumed his solidarity tour of Vancouver Island. The white New Westminster and North Arm members also appeared ready to break ranks, with each group setting its nets for a day before the militia's arrival. Worse, there was news that First Nations chiefs, angry at the lack of an acceptable settlement, were ready to head home and take their families with them. Without the First Nations women, many canneries would be crippled—but so would the union.

Nonetheless, the strikers could exert pressure. A few picket boats cruising the grounds at night could play havoc with the fleet, especially with the nets that could stretch hundreds of feet from their skiffs in conflicting tides and winds. Indeed, many reports of cut nets among the Nikkei fishers soon reached the authorities, incidents that MacLain airily attributed to late-night steamer movements. Even one hundred police, scattered on fishing grounds that stretched in an arc more than twenty kilometres from English Bay to Boundary Bay and upriver to New Westminster, were effectively powerless in their lumbering tugs against faster, nimbler picket boats. During the long hot July days, with Mount Baker a great white cone in the southeast, the Nikkei fishermen could watch one another, see strangers approach and provide mutual aid. Even during the moonless night of

July 24, the Fraser's waters were largely quiet. The struggle on the river remained a strike, not a civil war.

The union was down, but not out. The BCFU again reorganized the bargaining committee, again without Rogers, MacLain or J.H. Watson, who had been directing affairs in Vancouver. It is not clear how Indigenous fishers were represented, but it is hard to believe they were not included. First Nations' scrutineers had been prominent at the rejection vote and played a key role in fundraising and rallies. Rogers also insisted that only "bona fide fishermen" be allowed to attend future union meetings, a restriction designed to reinforce the authority of the union leadership. Despite the formal change, Rogers remained at the centre of events.

The union had time on its side. If Rogers could keep the remaining strikers united, a solution would have to be found at the bargaining table. Rumours that the sockeye run had begun in earnest were proving exaggerated. Even strike-breakers could not break a salmon strike if there were no salmon to be had.[117]

The legislature, now again in session, erupted in indignation with news of the militia's invasion of Steveston. The mobilization of the Duke of Connaught's Own Rifles may have complied with the letter of the law, but it had been organized by the canners to protect their own vested interests. Ralph Smith, a former miner and now a pro-labour member of the legislature for Nanaimo, took the lead in an emergency debate on the matter. Smith had already proposed a return to work pending binding arbitration, but neither fishermen nor canners were interested. A strong advocate of Asiatic exclusion and a vocal opponent of the Socialists, Smith had ostentatiously ignored MacLain, Kelly and their supporters when he encountered them during their solidarity tour to Nanaimo.

As the legislature debate raged on, Rogers and his committee took stock of the confrontation on the grounds. A large Nikkei fleet was fishing, it was true, but their catches were minimal and the canneries, denied the labour of First Nations women, could barely handle what was landed. The cannery workers had proved to be the key to the strike's continued effectiveness. If the union could hold back the rest of the fleet, it might yet secure a victory, or at least a draw.

The canners now sought to break away the Indigenous fishers. Duncan Bell-Irving summoned A.W. Vowell, superintendent of Indian Affairs, to join him in a meeting July 28 with leading chiefs at Canoe Pass, a hamlet on the Fraser's south shore near Steveston. Some agreed to fish the next day, according to news accounts, with a small group of Aboriginal fishers setting their nets near the North Pacific Cannery under cannery guard.[118] The strike also appeared to be fraying in New Westminster, where the union local had reportedly voted to accept nineteen cents. (This proved false.) But a union rally that day in Steveston showed that most white fishermen were determined to insist on a higher price and on union recognition. Rogers knew when to escalate and when to close the deal. He began to push for a settlement.

The union's Steveston headquarters was now a room in Harry Lee's Hotel, next door to a bar in the London Hotel where Rogers and MacLain could sometimes be found nursing beers.[119] Some meetings were held outdoors, but the more critical deliberations were held in the Steveston Opera House. The reporters for Carter-Cotton's *News-Advertiser* seemed to have been granted exclusive access to these closed gatherings, held in suffocating heat. Just a few blocks away, the militiamen swatted flies and attempted to maintain a veneer of military discipline. Negotiations in Steveston, supervised by E.P. Bremner, became continuous.

On July 28, nearly two weeks after the canners had confidently predicted an imminent union collapse, Rogers "laid it on the line to his members"—it was time to seek agreement. He sought approval of a counter-offer for a straight twenty cents a fish and union recognition. This improved on the Nikkei contract, he insisted, because it would eliminate in-season price cuts. He expressed concern for the plight of First Nations strikers if they lost the season and were forced to return to their homes empty-handed. When some militants objected, Rogers reminded them he had personally supported twenty cents some weeks before, but had respected the decision of the majority.

Bremner suddenly intervened by arriving with the news that the New Westminster fishermen had accepted a lesser offer of twenty cents a fish with a cut to fifteen cents in the event of a heavy run. It was useless to demand further concessions from the canners, Bremner declared, but Rogers urged the meeting to reject that advice and to insist on a straight twenty cents. The union men finally raised "a sea of sunburned hands" and unanimously agreed.

The talks now assumed even greater urgency. Francis Carter-Cotton had also travelled from Vancouver in an attempt to mediate, bringing Dr. Duncan Bell-Irving and William Farrell to represent the canners. Although he had not been re-elected as an MLA in the June election, Carter-Cotton's strong anti-Asian views made him acceptable to the fishermen as an intermediary (perhaps this was also the reason his *News-Advertiser* reporters were accorded access to BCFU meetings). All day Sunday the negotiations continued, sometimes with Bremner as mediator, sometimes with Carter-Cotton, sometimes with both sides face to face.

Although leadership of the Steveston fishermen had been restricted to "bona fide" fishermen, Rogers led the fishermen's three-man negotiating committee in Vancouver. For hours, no one moved. Finally, the BCFU committee blinked, proposing a straight season-long price of nineteen cents a fish. Rogers called a meeting to have this new counter-offer approved by the membership. The fishermen approved the new position by a three-to-one margin. A week had passed since the trumpets sounded to call out the militia, six days since the Nikkei fleet had set their nets. Fishing was about to begin for a second week. Yet the strike continued and the canners had been forced to return to the table to consider the new offer.[120]

Monday morning saw the entire executive committee of the FRCA gathered in Steveston. They blinked too. The letter they sent to Bremner accepted the nineteen cents proposal but pointedly ignored the demand for union recognition. The BCFU remained on strike until the canners formally ratified the offer later that afternoon. Despite the agreement, the BCFU members voted not to return to work until 6 a.m. Tuesday. They then elected Rogers president of their union and Will MacLain secretary, a strong reply to those who had accused the union men of being manipulated by outside radicals. News of Rogers's election was received with a standing ovation. The 1900 salmon strike was over. Carrier pigeons took the news to Nanaimo, and hundreds of excursionists from Vancouver and New Westminster travelled by steamer and launch to Steveston to watch the thousands of nets go into the water Sunday evening.[121]

In a report to Ottawa, E.P. Bremner declared the strike as the worst in the province in ten years. The settlement was more than the canners wanted, he concluded, but fishermen's compensation "for a possible two months in such an arduous occupation is much less than skilled craftsmen should receive." Despite an offer of a $100 reward for information on incidents of intimidation, only two arrests had been made.

The Sockeye Fusiliers folded their tents, filed onto the *Comox* and headed home, arriving in time to form an honour guard for a visiting dignitary. Their worst injuries were severe sunburns, although several reported dysentery. It was said the two militia companies consumed forty gallons of beer during their deployment. With talks nearing a conclusion, the soldiers had whiled away Saturday evening with musical performances and recitations. There was time for a church service before boarding the steamer at nine on Sunday morning. Worsnop began making efforts to find canners—or anyone—prepared to pay for the cost of the mobilization.[122]

Arguments quickly began over which settlement was superior. Was it the Nikkei contract of twenty cents a fish, with a cut to fifteen cents after six hundred? Or was it the straight BCFU price of nineteen cents? Fishermen calculated the breaking point at 725 fish. When weekly deliveries exceeded that number, the BCFU price was better. Below that number, the Nikkei fishermen came out ahead. But both sections of the fleet secured more than the canners' initial offer of fifteen cents, as well as a commitment to take all fish fit for processing and to apply weekly catch limits equally. Both also improved on the canners' amended position of twenty cents with a sliding scale or catch limits. The goal to hold the line before 1901's Big Year run had been achieved, but there were more far-reaching judgements that would shape the future of the Nikkei community in profound ways.

Nikkei accounts of the settlement took a longer view. "The Japanese should not be called strike-breakers," declared Dantai's official history. "It was clear to everyone that the canneries could not possibly pay twenty-five cents apiece. Our decision to start fishing for twenty cents resulted in our victory and the development of Steveston as the residence of our people."[123] This conclusion, written in 1935, just six years before the wartime expulsion of the Nikkei from BC, was tragically optimistic. Pressure against the Nikkei was growing, not waning, in the days after the settlement. On August 7, 1900, in response to pressure from Ottawa, the Japanese government suspended emigration to Canada. A few weeks after fishing began, the BC legislature passed an anti-immigration bill that was to set the tone for a generation of racist legislation directed at Asians of all backgrounds.[124]

Undeterred, Tomekichi Homma sought to register to vote in Vancouver on October 19. Registrar Thomas Cunningham sternly turned him away, opening the way for the legal test Homma had hoped would follow. He had his day in court November 29, when the registrar's decision was overturned. Cunningham was defiant. "Courts or no courts, orders or no orders," Asiatics would not be allowed to vote, Cunningham vowed. Attorney General Eberts immediately appealed the lower court decision and in March, defeated once more, he sought leave to appeal to the Privy Council in London. In Victoria, the government worked on every front to limit Chinese and Japanese immigration. During that fall, Eberts investigated charges of fraudulent immigration practices that allowed newly landed Nikkei fishermen to receive naturalization papers through the mail within months of arrival. When BC sent a senior government delegation to Ottawa in October, Chinese and Japanese immigration was the first order of business in talks with Laurier and his officials.[125]

Soon after the strike, thirty-nine canners gathered in Vancouver to consider their options. Further amalgamation seemed essential to control the costs and risks of the salmon fishery but W.D. Burdis, the new secretary of the FRCA, set to work devising less drastic measures to strengthen their hand without forcing a fundamental change. For the moment, most preferred to await the Big Year and its promise of staggering profits.[126]

The BCFU continued its organizing activities in the wake of the settlement. Striking railway workers hailed MacLain during a strike rally late in August and the Port Simpson band, still in Steveston, entertained fishers and cannery workers at a command performance the same week.[127] As the runs began to dwindle in late August of 1900, Rogers took the steamer to Victoria where a special committee of the legislature had been convened to inquire into the events of the summer. The hearings were driven by Eberts but chaired by R.G. Tatlow, a Vancouver real estate magnate whose business was housed in the Henry Bell-Irving Building at Richards and Cordova.

During four days of hearings, the legislators grilled police officers, justices of the peace, a canner, a Nikkei fisherman named Oki and a Musqueam fisher whose name was not recorded. Throughout the testimony, MacLain emerged as the radical firebrand and Rogers as the dealmaker.

Robert Whiteside, a justice of the peace and cannery foreman at Pacific Coast Packing, said he had seen Brown roughed up on the dock and heard MacLain tell strikers of a huge solidarity meeting at Nanaimo's Extension Mine, where the miners had pledged their support. "If you men will only hang on a day or two longer," MacLain cried, "we will have barrels of money and shiploads of provisions and not only that but the miners have pledged themselves to give you their support by coming here in a body two thousand strong." By comparison, Rogers never made "inflammatory speeches," cannery owner C.S. Windsor claimed. Rogers had privately welcomed the militia as the only thing that averted violence, Windsor said, adding, "[Rogers] and I got along very nicely together; he's a man that's got a good deal of sense." Windsor was adamant the Nikkei had won the best price in the summer's negotiations.

With the inquiry drawing to a close, Richmond MLA Thomas Kidd, a farmer, then walked Rogers through his testimony. The socialist union leader who many blamed for the entire dispute answered the questions briefly and factually, describing his efforts throughout the summer to achieve a negotiated settlement. The turning point had been the sudden decision of the Nikkei to abandon the united front to achieve twenty-five cents. "They told us they would stand firm with the union until the canners proved to the whole of us that they could not afford to pay twenty-five cents; and then, probably, we would come to some other agreement." The union left nothing to chance, making regular visits to the Nikkei bunkhouses to urge them to hold firm. By agreement with Dantai, Nikkei boats would patrol to keep the Nikkei fleet tied up and union boats would focus on white fishermen, but carry a Nikkei interpreter "so that when we came across a Jap fishing we would be able to tell him." But the Nikkei reversal had come without warning.

When the militia arrived and most of the Nikkei fleet had set their nets, there was talk that the union "would ask the whites and Indians to go home," Rogers said, but 250 Nikkei remained loyal to the strike and even "tried to induce their own men not to go fishing." There was no likelihood of widespread violence, if only because Nikkei fishers outnumbered whites and Indigenous fishers by three or four to one. A union committee of safety was appointed to monitor the picketing and "everything went on smoothly ... We told the men that they would not accomplish anything by violence—that it would only hurt our cause."

With that, the inquiry ended and the special committee wound up its affairs. The finger of blame pointed at "a rough element" from across the border, the committee told the legislature, a reference to American interlopers or "certain agitators" that had barely been mentioned in hours of testimony. The bottom line: no evidence whatsoever was produced that the provincial government was in any way involved in calling out the militia, and it was therefore not liable either financially or politically.

The mood in the province was lightening. The Labour Day parade held September 3 in Vancouver began its march around the city from city hall, at what is now Main and Hastings, with two fishermen's floats, a firefighters' float, floats displaying union-made goods, and "native war dances" performed by the Port Simpson men "in their Indian costume." Photos of the parade show Tsimshian men, wearing cedar neck rings, moccasins and richly designed woollen blankets, marching down a sun-drenched street as onlookers applaud and children run alongside. The "smoking concert" that night featured "innumerable features, songs, speeches, recitations." Sports Day at Brockton Oval included gillnetter races in Burrard Inlet. It was a high-water mark for the BC Fishermen's Union members, who just five weeks earlier had seemed on the brink of a devastating defeat.[128]

Soon after, First Nations fishers and their families dispersed, some to the hop fields of the Fraser Valley, others to sawmills in Puget Sound. By mid-autumn, all would return to their home communities. For chiefs heading home for the season, the news of Japan's August decision to clamp down on emigration to North America may have seemed like an answer to their demands, although it did nothing to reduce the numbers of Nikkei fishermen already in British Columbia. The influx of Nikkei entering the province would drop from more than nine thousand in 1900 to just eleven hundred a year later and provincial legislation to impose a language test on those seeking fishing licences would add to the new restrictions. Aboriginal leaders, however, wanted both more access and a better price.[129]

The DCOR members sent to South Africa a year earlier had arrived in time for the Battle of Paardeberg, where the inexperienced troops had suffered many casualties but helped turn the tide in a pivotal battle. The Dukes had seen the relief of Mafeking and the fall of Pretoria before embarking for their return to Canada. Defeat of the Boers and victory for the Empire now seemed certain. Their train pulled into Vancouver on New Year's Eve, 1900, to a rapturous reception, and when the New Westminster volunteers finally reached home, the city celebrated with a "perfect blaze of rockets," issuing each veteran a gold watch and closing Columbia Street for a massive parade.[130]

CHAPTER 7

CIVIL WAR

The 1900 strike cost the canners a significant loss of production, perhaps as much as fifty thousand cases of salmon with a wholesale value of $200,000. On that score, the BCFU could claim a victory, denying the canners a large share of the pack and averting a much larger cut in the price of salmon. But the canners emerged from the struggle largely unscathed, poorer but wiser. They had learned important lessons from confrontation in 1900, most importantly that nothing, not even the militia, could guarantee peace on the fishing grounds. Unable to manage violence, they decided to embrace it, using the Nikkei as their agents.

Confidential internal agreements were implemented to reduce the numbers, and hence the leverage, of the non-Nikkei fleet. A rating system was created, allocating a fixed number of boats to each cannery, to pool the catch and control the overall size of the fleet. Decision-making was delegated to a seven-member executive and a three-member working group, although Bell-Irving no doubt held an effective veto. The canners agreed to bind each fisherman to an individual cannery and to regulate the price of salmon to eliminate competition on the grounds. The agreements extended to the sale of the pack as well, with the FRCA members agreeing to fight for cheaper rail freight rates and to create a new combine to control the sale of the pack in the United Kingdom. By late June of 1901, FRCA secretary W.D. Burdis was able to advise the canners that the overall fleet size had been set at 3,108 boats. It was highly doubtful that union militants would have access to those gillnetters.[131]

The canners also took steps to avoid a repeat of the Sockeye Fusiliers fiasco. The militia would be unavailable a second time—Worsnop had not managed to secure payment for his services from the Richmond town council—and had proved useless in any case. Contemptuous of the abilities of the province's special constables, Bell-Irving and his colleagues decided to look among the fishermen themselves for someone capable of protecting strikebreaking fishermen in the face of union pickets. They needed a strategist, someone fluent in Nikkei, English and Chinook, and unafraid of violence. The best candidate was obvious: Yasushi Yamazaki.

Yamazaki quickly changed allegiances. He resigned from Dantai's executive and took charge of policing the grounds. Deputized by both provincial and local authorities—in effect, the canners—he created armed patrols for the Fraser, available to provide quick and effective protection to Nikkei fishers confronting union pickets. Although Dantai would continue to bargain with the canners, and strike until a satisfactory offer was received, Yamazaki's career change must have confirmed for many white and Indigenous fishermen that the Nikkei fleet was bought and paid for by the canners. Then and later, the Dantai leadership considered their success in 1900 a turning point for the community, a milestone in their struggle to establish a foothold in their new homeland. Many union and First Nations fishers drew the opposite conclusion: that the effectiveness of Dantai showed the need to redouble efforts for Asiatic exclusion.[132]

Throughout the spring of 1901, however, Caucasians and Nikkei in Steveston lived in harmony. On May 25, the white community held a field day with horse races that delighted the hundreds of Nikkei residents lining the track. The Nikkei boatmen carried off the trophy for the races on the Fraser.[133]

The union had consolidated its organization during the winter. A strike committee formed on June 10 selected Frank Rogers, still president, and Charles Durham, a fisherman from the last year's executive, to be public spokesmen, an assignment Rogers would have cause to regret. MacLain had left the union leadership to pursue his political ambitions, adding his voice to a civic controversy over a proposal to build a music hall where alcohol might be served (MacLain was in favour).[134]

In early April, Rogers wrote a long letter to the editor of the *News-Advertiser* that demonstrated how much he had fallen under the spell of the salmon, although he had never been a fisherman, and how much he had broadened his perspective beyond labour or even political considerations. In a key passage, which came after a declaration that the canners were wasting one fish for every one they canned, he wrote:

> There is reason for believing ... the salmon are slowly but surely being exterminated. One instance is that the fisherman goes farther out in the Gulf to fish

than several years ago, and such a wall of nets is cast outside the river that the fish become frightened and keep farther away, and the closed hours are so few that before the fish venture near the river, nearly half of the close limit has expired.

Now, sir, why I refer to these matters is that I believe no person or persons have a just right to waste the resources of any country, whether they be fishermen or canners. We owe something to the coming generations and our duty is to hand down to them the resources of a country in a proper state, not history which will tell them that the people of this age exploited and wasted the food supply—nature's gift to mankind—for the greed of gold.

It is, sir, unfortunate to refer to this question. But the truth will always prevail. We have the history of the buffalo, which roamed the mighty prairies. Men said, "You cannot kill them all." That those mighty herds would not be destroyed.

But Alas! What do we find today? Almost any child can tell the result of man's destruction. And again what has become of those wonderful pine forests of the States of Wisconsin and Michigan?

Now, sir, knowing these facts to be true, I make a plea for the salmon before it is too late. I find no personal fault with the canners or fishermen on this side of the line, or in the United States, and I might say I am aware of how destructive the traps are on the American side.

My contention is that it is the function and the duty of a government of the whole of the people to protect the resources of a country for the benefit of all the people, and not allow the resources to be wasted and destroyed by a few of the people for greed. And if a government will not carry out that duty, that government should not try and govern.

And in conclusion, sir, if any public-spirited citizen thinks I am right in making my plea for the protection of the salmon, and believes we are not the last people to live on this earth, but that the children growing up now should have the resources after we are gone and that history would not read better saying that our forefathers were partly civilized and did not quite destroy all that was in sight, it is that citizen's duty to use his efforts to save the salmon before it is too late, too late, too late. I believe in a system by which when you cut a tree down, you plant a tree to grow in its place.[135]

This emotional, passionate letter, written between the events of 1900 and 1901, makes an argument that is as valid today as it was then—with no mention of race. Despite the Nikkei actions of 1900, Rogers had evidently not given up on uniting the fishermen of all races, but his letter went far beyond collective bargaining. This mysterious man, who came out of nowhere to lead the BCFU in what had been the biggest strike in the province's history, was challenging all "public-spirited citizens," regardless of class, to consider the future, their children, and not just the possibilities of short-term personal profit. He was challenging the under-pinnings of BC's economy. Apparently Rogers—political campaigner, union organizer, socialist ideologue, pragmatic negotiator, rank-and-file leader, environmentalist—was also a philosopher.

In this respect, at least, he had much in common with Yamazaki. Did the two men, both seafarers, ever compare notes over a beer? Or seek to rationalize or understand Dantai's sudden settlement? The price agreed to by Dantai, after all, was the one Rogers had privately thought most realistic from the beginning. Was Yamazaki working behind the scenes to keep the Dantai leadership aligned with the union, as he dutifully repeated their commitment to unity at conferences with skeptical union leaders? Or was he keeping a smokescreen up while others closed the deal? How was Rogers able to hold back the anti-Japanese forces in his union—not least the Indigenous leaders—who made no secret of their contempt for Dantai's members? Once Yamazaki had signed up with the canners, of course, any communication would be risky. Any contact before Yamazaki's move would have been seen as naïve by the membership, any contact afterward as a sign of betrayal. Yet Rogers, driven by the realization that a strike without Nikkei support was practically doomed to fail, tried to make the connection. He once again began meeting with JFBA leaders.

Five locals were now organized under the banner of the BCFU's Grand Lodge: Vancouver, New Westminster, Eburne, Canoe Pass and the ever-reliable Port Simpson. Who spoke for the Lax Kw'alaams people in the lodge, however, was not clear. During the winter, George Kelly had moved permanently to Port Simpson, apparently at the urging of Diex, his adoptive mother. A prolonged crisis in the Lax Kw'alaams leadership, which would result in Kelly receiving the storied name of Lige'ex several years later, was gripping the Tsimshian community.[136]

Then, with the Big Year run just weeks away, First Nations leaders took steps to assert their power. During the first week of June, First Nations chiefs from the Skeena River to the Fraser Canyon gathered in Chilliwack to discuss the coming season. Thirty-three chiefs signed a petition to the union declaring they would "not go to the canneries until the offer to fish for fifteen cents is accepted," a reduced-price demand that reflected the enormous volumes expected in the Big Year run. The "huge assemblage" in Chilliwack was unprecedented in a province where the non-Indigenous population was at its lowest level in the wake of smallpox and countless other assaults. In the same period, the non-Indigenous population had exploded. The Chilliwack meeting was newsworthy both by its size and its single-minded focus on the salmon fishery. Although newspaper reports were scant, it was known that the chiefs had summoned Captain J.L. Anderson, the union's most long-serving officer, to hear their demands and to receive their pledge of support for the union. Anderson agreed on united action to achieve the fifteen-cent demand with regard to the price for sockeye. The chiefs added ominously that "the whites need not bother about the Japs, they would look after them."[137]

The chiefs were angry. The 1900 struggle had not advanced them one step closer to their goal of restoring their access to the sockeye by reducing and eliminating the Nikkei fleet. The previous year's strike had focused on economic demands—and recognition of the union—not the political challenge of restoring Indigenous participation in the salmon fishery. Yet without First Nations support, the union effort would have been crippled. The Lax Kw'alaams contingent, with its brass band and firm union commitment, had not only led fundraising efforts and brightened every rally with its music, but had joined forces with the most militant elements of the labour movement, participating in meetings at the United Socialist Labour Party hall.

This solidarity, often acknowledged by MacLain and Rogers, had not been reflected in the leadership of the strike. Although Kelly's demand for Nikkei exclusion had dominated

the speeches at the July 14, 1900, Vancouver strike rally—
where the speakers included the likes of Joseph Martin and
Socialist party firebrand Ernest Burns—other Aboriginal
leaders were seldom in evidence, nor was there any sign
they were included in key negotiations or strategy sessions.
Indigenous fishermen helped supervise the balloting at the
critical July 19 rejection vote, suggesting that First Nations
fishers participated in the union on the basis of full equality.
Inclusion at the rank-and-file level did not seem to extend
to the leadership, though Rogers often referred to the enormous effort required to restrain Indigenous leaders from
violent reprisals against the Nikkei. MacLain and Anderson
often paid tribute to the militancy of the First Nations fleet,
but only MacLain seems to have spent much time working
directly with the Lax Kw'alaams fishers, largely on fundraising and morale-building tours.

Opposition to Nikkei participation in the fishery—or
any other part of BC society—had not waned. The union's
Vancouver local kept a steady stream of telegrams and letters
flowing to Ottawa, demanding a crackdown on the fraudulent naturalization papers being issued to recent Nikkei
arrivals. On March 8, 1901, Homma's appeal of his rejection from the voters list was heard in Vancouver amid angry
press coverage. The union's efforts to build bridges with the
Japanese Fishermen's Benevolent Society leadership in 1900
were an exception to the rule.

Public opinion was overwhelmingly anti-Asiatic, especially in the labour movement. Vancouver's papers were
providing blanket coverage in May 1901 to the hearings
of a national Royal Commission into "Oriental Labour."
Bell-Irving and canner Frank Burnett, who opposed restrictions on Asian immigrants, testified for several hours, with
Burnett conceding that "sentimentally he was in favour of

Oriental restriction, but from a purely business point of view he was not." Apart from the canners, who chose their words carefully—Bell-Irving declared himself in favour of "free trade in labour for some time to come"—no one could be found to oppose expulsion of the Nikkei.[138]

Union fisherman George Mackie, a member of the New Westminster local, told the commission that if the Nikkei continued to arrive in large numbers, "I will either have to leave or to starve. Circumstances cannot [get] better with these people here. The Mongolians have cut me out of everything as well as they have done in the fishing. I have applied at various places, at sawmills and factories, for employment, and cannot get it. During the three years I have been here I have only been able to secure work for four months outside of the fisheries." The commission heard from anyone who wished to appear, carefully transcribing the testimony of scores of witnesses, including many fishermen, in days of hearings. Only the New Westminster local sent official representatives. If Frank Rogers had wished to show leadership on this issue, dear to his members' hearts, he had a perfect opportunity. He did not appear.[139]

But the First Nations chiefs did not miss their chance. Chief James Harry of the Squamish First Nation spoke for three other Squamish chiefs as well as Chief Casino of Langley and Chief James Isaac of Port Hammond:

> The Japanese come to this country, they come too thick altogether. It don't matter where you go, you see Japanese. You go to the Fraser River, you see Japanese, hundreds in the summer time. You go to Howe Sound, nothing but Japanese. You go to Indian River, just the same, nothing but Japanese. In fishing time we had no chance to fish ourselves ... People

have no chance to make a living. Can't make bread and butter ... They began about three years ago and get thicker, thicker, thicker all the time, and last year too thick altogether.[140]

There was no sign that white fishermen sought elimination of the Nikkei as a way to restore Indigenous rights, or that they were even aware of a "land question," as Indigenous leaders called their struggle for acknowledgement of their rights and title. The support of First Nations fishers was welcome and the anger of Indigenous leaders at the rise of the Nikkei fleet easy to understand, but at no point did union leaders propose affirmative action on behalf of First Nations fishers. It seemed to have been taken for granted that the purpose of Nikkei exclusion was to preserve the fishery for white fishers.

Despite the chasm that now divided white and Nikkei fishermen, Rogers sought once more to engage with the Nikkei leaders, convinced that only united action would produce enough pressure on the canners to win a settlement.

The 1900 confrontation had been anticipated by all as a rehearsal for the Big Year run of 1901, with all sides making frantic preparations months ahead of time. Now, with the Big Year prize in sight, some of the combatants seemed complacent—or resigned. The canners, their strategic changes already implemented, were distracted by a provincial attempt to take over jurisdiction of the fishery, a legislative initiative that Watson denounced, on behalf of the fishermen, as a sellout to the canners. There would be no need for such sweeping legislation, he said, if the canners would hire white fishermen only.[141]

The union leaders believed they had won a form of union recognition in 1900 with their face-to-face negotiations with the canners. In fact, there was every indication that the canners would negotiate in that fashion again. If Rogers, now president, was making special preparations for a confrontation, there was no sign of it in newspaper reports. Always the strategist, he must have been aware that the fishermen's leverage was much weakened by the increasing strength of the Nikkei fleet, the consolidation of Dantai and the size of the Big Year runs, which made price considerations much less important. No one wanted to miss the Big Year.

All these considerations no doubt played a role in the formulation of the price demands. Although Rogers had personally favoured a twenty-cent opening demand in 1900, as did many of the Nikkei bosses, all three sections of the fleet had endorsed a twenty-five-cent opening position and bargained down from there. In 1901, all three sections opened with a "final" position. When Anderson met with the chiefs in Chilliwack, he had no problem agreeing to fifteen cents, even though it was far below the settlement price in 1900. In fact, the union leaders were tabling a fifteen-cent demand to the canners that same day in Vancouver.

Wary of losing fishing time and determined to bring matters to an early conclusion, the canners tabled an opening position of twelve cents with a drop to ten cents if the run was particularly heavy. This was a far cry from the ten-cent gap that had been a feature of bargaining a year earlier. The *Vancouver Daily World*, a reliable barometer of the canners' thinking, emphasized the difficulties in world markets and the need for an attitude of compromise. The estimated fifty thousand cases of production that the forty-three canneries had lost from the 1900 strike occurred in a year when the total pack was only 161,243 cases. The canners, despite their preparations for a strike, were also keen to avoid more lost production.

The fishermen were clearly anxious to bargain. By June 17, the BCFU had dropped its demand to 12.5 cents throughout the season, although there were rumours the Nikkei were ready to accept an in-season drop to ten cents to avoid lost fishing time. A Nikkei contractor named Okani, claiming to represent two thousand fishermen, went even further. His fleet would fish for ten cents season-long, he declared, provided there were no limits on their weekly landings. And a June 15 meeting of the Nikkei bosses had agreed on 12.5 cents to August 3 but ten cents thereafter.[142]

Negotiations stalled, however, on June 19 when the canners made their "final" offer of 12.5 cents with a weekly limit of only two hundred fish. Once that number was caught, the price would drop to an unspecified level. Two hundred was a very small number for a Big Year fishery. Rogers repeated the demand for 12.5 cents season-long without limits, claiming the support of 90 percent of the Nikkei. But voices from the Nikkei fleet continued to suggest a settlement was near, especially if the two-hundred-fish limit was not imposed until later in the season. Later that day, the canners made another effort to win a settlement with the Nikkei, proposing 12.5 cents a fish until July 27, when the limit of two hundred would be imposed only in the event of a larger-than-expected run; even then, the canners promised they would take "all they can handle."

According to the *World*, it was "understood that all the little brown men on the river will agree." In fact, news reports that day confirmed that the Nikkei had settled, but with a 250-fish limit. The canners promised, as well, to guarantee the Nikkei any higher price extracted by the BCFU. The canners then made a further move, announcing their new boat rating system to reduce the fleet to 3,108 boats from

4,000. The union countered with a demand for strict limits on the size of the Nikkei fleet.[143]

Although Rogers claimed he had again been able to secure a commitment from the JFBA not to fish before a union settlement, he was dealing with new Dantai leadership—and not necessarily those actually in charge of the negotiations. The Nikkei bosses were again playing a critical background role. The Fraser River Canners' Association had taken active steps during the winter to strengthen their connections to Dantai and its leaders, who were confronting a host of difficult challenges. The Homma challenge was consuming significant legal resources and construction of the Steveston hospital had been financed with loans. The needs of the fishermen were great, but the cash requirements of the community leadership were even greater. In 1900, Rogers had spent weeks in Steveston meeting Nikkei leaders, interviewing sympathetic canners and connecting with First Nations chiefs. In 1901, Rogers found that the canners were there far ahead of him, with incomparably greater resources, to build their own relationship with the Nikkei.

Behind the scenes, Burdis had convinced FRCA members to close the deal with a secret advance payment to Dantai of three dollars a man "to use for the hospital, subject to the signing of a contract." In a private and confidential memo to FRCA members, Burdis urged "that the canners accede to this request as it was the hope of receiving this assistance which induced the Japanese to so quickly come to our terms. Last year there was a large amount of sickness amongst the Jap fishermen and ... in case of death, the hospital pays all funeral expenses. The committee believes the hospital to be doing good work and is an institution deserving of support."[144]

This secret payment, which triggered a Nikkei settlement June 20 on the canners' terms, was equivalent to about two days' wages for each fisherman, an irresistible lure to Nikkei bosses who had advanced several thousand dollars from their own resources to build the hospital. The total amount of the payment is not known, but could have risen to as much as $10,000 if boat pullers were included as well as fishermen. The advance, if it was ever repaid, could easily have been recouped by the bosses with special charges against the accounts of the individual fishermen. It is not surprising that contractors like Okani would insist on settling, even at a lower price, when the possibility of a windfall payment of hundreds of dollars was dangled before them.[145]

The Nikkei settlement was a double blow to Rogers: his efforts at unity with the Nikkei had been repudiated in humiliating fashion—many said for a second time, remembering 1900—and the union's bargaining power was dramatically weakened. There was talk among the First Nations fishers of going logging if a better price could not be achieved. They insisted they would "not fish, nor allow their Klootchmen to work if 12 ½ cents is not given throughout." (Klootchman was the Chinook word for "woman" or "wife.") It was a sign of the importance of this commitment that Anderson and Rogers now took a First Nations representative, always a chief, to key meetings.[146]

With no fish in the river yet, the decision of the Nikkei fishers was of little immediate significance. On June 23, the union locals had affirmed their determination of a flat price of 12.5 cents and a limit on imports of trap fish. Rogers, Anderson and a First Nations chief presented that position to Board of Trade officers on June 25, the only occasion when the participation of a First Nations leader on the negotiating team is documented (his name was not reported).[147]

But the union fishermen revealed their apprehension about a strike at a "mass meeting" in Vancouver on June 26. This time there were no marches around the city, no Nelson's Cornet Band. The fishermen and their sympathizers gathered "to lay before the citizens their grievances" in the city's Market Hall, the ornate two-storey brick building with an upstairs theatre at Main and Hastings that served as city hall. For the first time, the option of binding arbitration won serious consideration.

Anderson led off, declaring that the problems of the industry would persist "as long as the Dominion Government allowed the Japanese to flood the labour market." He did a lengthy breakdown of the canners' costs, concluding that even allowing "one dollar per case for wine and fast horses and sleepless nights," a canner could still expect to double an investment of $20,000 in a single season.

Then it was Rogers's turn. The Nikkei fleet was now large enough to supply the canners without the catches of the union fleet, Rogers warned. The union had once again sought a united front with the Nikkei fleet and won a commitment that their boats would remain tied up until the union had won a price. "The Grand Lodge appreciated the value of the Japs' help and the Japanese had given their word of honour that they would stand with the white fishermen." But the Japanese Fishermen's Benevolent Association had now settled, and 60 percent of the Nikkei fleet was now preparing to fish. "The white men had tried to bring the Japs up to their level and now the latter were trying to drag the white men down." He paid tribute to the solidarity of the First Nations, hoping there would be no basis for the Indigenous fishers to say "cultus white men"—meaning "worthless," "useless," "evil" or "taboo" in Chinook.

With that, Capilano Chief Jimmy Harry took the podium to pledge the support of First Nations fishermen. "He had nothing to say of the Japanese," the *World* reported, "but wanted to know why they did not stay in their own country. The Indians and whites must stand as one." At one time "the Indians owned the whole country, river and everything," Chief Harry reminded his audience. "No trouble then and no strike." Not surprisingly, a motion endorsing the fishermen's position passed unanimously and the crowd then adjourned "in as orderly a fashion as if it were a prayer meeting breaking up." If there was a Pinkerton man in the crowd, he had little to report.[148]

The Market Hall meeting proved that the possibility of organizing across race lines, if it had ever existed, had been lost. Even Rogers, who had carefully refrained from appeals to race in 1900, now made expulsion of the Nikkei the key to his bargaining strategy. With the Nikkei fleet now fishing before the rest of the fishermen for the second year in a row, he had little practical alternative. George Kelly's discordant speech of 1900 was now the common-sense view in 1901, and the consequences of this deep antagonism between Indigenous and Nikkei communities would be dire, as thoughtful leaders of the Nikkei community later realized. The decision to fish, producing an apparent victory at the time, set in motion a struggle for survival that the Nikkei community proved unable to win.

The labour movement's attention was elsewhere, in any case, focused on a prolonged strike of CPR trackmen, the labourers who walked twelve to fourteen kilometres of track a day to do maintenance, summer and winter, for $1.25 per day. The CPR strike was national in scope and the Vancouver papers carried daily appeals from strikers in remote parts of the province denouncing the CPR and expressing their determination to win a raise. For these men too, Asian labour was a major preoccupation, but divisions among the various railway-running trades—the Brotherhood of Locomotive Engineers refused to endorse strike action by anyone— made their struggle even more difficult. With Vancouver's economy dependent on the CPR, the intermittent interruption of freight service by strike action was more worrisome than a strike on the Fraser, where the anticipated size of the run made price considerations seem marginal.[149]

It is not clear why there was no settlement, given the narrow differences between the canners and the union. E.P. Bremner calculated that each side would have to concede less than eight-tenths of a cent a fish to land on the same spot, equivalent to about $1,000 per cannery for the season. On the union side, this represented about $22 per boat, only $11 per man. But Bremner was working in the realm of pragmatism. For the canners, this was a chance to break the union once and for all, using the strength of the Nikkei fishermen to do the heavy lifting. For the fishermen, ideals, prejudices and dreams were in play: for the First Nations, the right to fish; for the Nikkei, the right to equality; for the whites, union recognition and the vindication of forcing the canners to yield. For each section of the fleet, the positive ideal had its negative counterpart: for the whites and the First Nations, the goal of expelling the Nikkei; for the Nikkei, the right to remain. Short of a union surrender, which was unlikely until the run arrived, the canners could end the confrontation for a pittance. They chose to continue.

When the canners refused to respond to the BCFU's new proposal, the union membership met once more on June 30 to set midnight as a strike deadline. A last-ditch canners' offer to lift the two-hundred-fish limit when paying the ten-cent price was brushed off. The fishermen demanded union recognition, condemning the individual contracts sought by the canners as a form of union-busting. There

would be no settlement at less than 12.5 cents for the duration of the season. The union was on strike once again, this
time a week earlier than in 1900. The early deadline was a
sign of the membership's desire to avoid lost fishing time. So
far, there was no sign of the sockeye.[150]

The Nikkei fishermen remained tied up in the early
days of the strike, in part because there were no fish, in part
because of the threat of violence. A meeting of Dantai leaders
on Monday, July 2, resulted in a decision to postpone any
concerted effort to fish until the following Sunday. If anyone
harboured any doubts about Dantai's decision to settle,
they kept them to themselves, no doubt recalling the harsh
discipline meted out to dissidents in 1900. With few fish in
the river, there was no reason to risk a confrontation. As a
result, most of the Nikkei fleet remained tied up for more
than a week after the Dantai settlement. Two crews that
did try to fish on July 7 were badly beaten by union pickets.
The next night, the vanguard of the run was in the river. At
least one hundred boats left the docks—a fraction of the
fleet—escorted by twenty-six armed patrol boats. Yamazaki's
preparations would be put to the test.

The *Albion* was the flagship of Yamazaki's fleet, a
one-hundred-foot tugboat launched just two years earlier
for Albion cannery. Capable in any weather, the tug had
ample accommodation for Yamazaki's armed crew, which
boarded the *Albion* each day at dawn and patrolled the
Fraser, the North Arm and as far north as English Bay and
Point Atkinson before returning to Steveston in the early
hours of the morning. When the Nikkei fleet set its nets
July 8, Yamazaki had twenty-three patrol boats in Steveston
and three on the North Arm, each crewed by eight to fifteen
armed fishermen. Union pickets, when they were spotted,
were often chased into Canoe Pass, the meandering channel

on the south side of the Fraser's main stem, where the union had established its own picket fleet near Ladner. Yamazaki's diary recorded long hours of tedious and uneventful patrolling, but there were many incidents that confirmed Rogers's forecast of violence.

On July 8, the *World* reported violent clashes on the Fraser. The previous day at Terra Nova, the North Arm community where Musqueam fishers were based, "the Indians were out in their big war canoes and it would have fared ill with any Japanese who made an attempt to fish." Union members from New Westminster travelled down to Steveston to "stop anyone who attempted to fish and it was not suggested that they would be any too gentle about it," whether the strikebreakers were Nikkei or white. But no one set a net until dusk, when a single Nikkei gillnetter began fishing within sight of the Gulf of Georgia cannery. A picket boat swooped down to intervene, boatloads of Nikkei and white fishermen rushed out to assist, and a confrontation seemed imminent. But the Nikkei fishermen soon picked up their net and returned to shore, insisting they were only food fishing. On the North Arm, however, two incidents occurred "with sticks, oars and clubs," which ended with five Nikkei beaten senseless. Dantai's leaders later estimated there were fifty police aboard fifteen boats to provide protection to those fishing, each boat receiving ten dollars per day. This number was soon increased to twenty-five boats.[151]

The next day was quiet, with the monotony broken by reports that Chinese cannery workers were threatening to strike in support of the BCFU. Another day passed without the threatened mass fishery by the Nikkei. The provincial superintendent of police found Steveston so quiet that he decided no special constables would be required. The *World* reporter counted about three hundred union pickets in about fifty boats, each with a union burgee bearing the letter *U*, impressive but hardly enough to hold back several thousand Nikkei fishermen. Given the imbalance, he concluded, "it is not difficult to see that the Japanese have the river." The main reason there was little fishing was obvious: so far, there were still few fish.

When Yamazaki did find it necessary to apprehend a union supporter, the consequences could be severe. Those caught were supposed to be taken to police court in Vancouver, but Yamazaki found this too restrictive. He re-established his own JFBA "private court," according to one of his biographers, where white fishermen were compelled to pay compensation for their interference with Nikkei fishers. Yamazaki's jurisdiction expanded far beyond the fishery. Even domestic issues like love triangles might be adjudicated in his court, where the judge laboured late into the night before relaxing with sake. It must have been terrifying for a white fisherman to be arraigned before Yamazaki, who was no doubt supported by a group of tough, dedicated deputies, and never let his revolver out of his sight.[152]

Day after day, the number of Nikkei fishers increased. Was Yamazaki regulating the flow of boats to the grounds? His work was simplified by the relatively few Nikkei boats setting their nets. Were there still "old-time Japs" who would have preferred to stand with the union? That option had disappeared.

The clashes continued as the strike entered its second week. By July 9, most of the Nikkei fleet was at sea, the whites on the Fraser "in a minority," although reports continued of significant support among the Nikkei for the union position. Some divisions may have remained among the Nikkei, but Rogers's most feared outcome had been realized. The Nikkei were fishing in sufficient numbers to render the BCFU strike irrelevant. Nikkei deliveries had to be cut off if the union was to survive. The Nikkei fishermen would not return to the docks without a credible and immediate threat. The union needed some dramatic escalation to avoid collapse. Rogers and his executive decided to execute a desperate and risky plan. Any pretence of unity across race lines was cast aside.

The BCFU organized another mass meeting on July 10 at which the membership resolved that "every member should pledge himself to aid in driving the Japanese off the river." Rogers told *Province* reporter R.W. Brown that some of the canners had advanced money to the Japanese to purchase rifles and revolvers, and had "ordered the Japs when they shoot, they must shoot to kill. The fishermen consider this arming of the Japs a step which means civil war. And the fishermen will ask all white men and Indians to govern themselves accordingly." The union took steps to deploy sixty boats on the fishing grounds in an effort to shut down fishing. By July 11, with catches rising to two hundred fish per boat, the first reports of gunfire filled the papers.[153]

This was the second "shoot to kill" order on the Fraser. Worsnop had given the same command a year earlier. Although Rogers claimed that union pickets would not be armed, he warned that a settlement would come only with a season-long fixed price and preferential hiring for union members. Burdis denied that the canners had provided arms to anyone. Picketing intensified. Weapons were seized and thrown overboard, nets cut, boats destroyed. Terrorized Nikkei fishermen were left stranded on isolated beaches. Yamazaki's men told him seven Nikkei fishermen were missing and unaccounted for, some feared dead.[154]

Day after day, the deadly game continued. Tugs towed small fleets of steam launches, crowded with union fishermen, to the fishing grounds. The picket boats ran interference between Yamazaki's fleet of armed men and the Nikkei gillnetters who were brave enough to set their nets. As darkness fell, the conflict was joined in earnest. Gunfire flashed amid groups of picket boats setting upon isolated gillnetters who were· struggling to land the first sockeye of what promised to be a record-breaking run.

On the night of July 10, the crew of the *Albion* heard gunfire off Point Grey. Yamazaki was in charge, with Ichitaro Suzuki, Iwakichi Imamura and Kamekichi Ohki, one of the most powerful men in Dantai. All were armed with pistols. Their lights revealed a battered boat on a Point Grey beach, with blood on the floorboards but no fishermen in sight. (None was ever found.) Yamazaki ordered the police on board the *Albion* to hide under tarpaulins on the deck as they continued into English Bay. He hoped to spring a trap on Rogers to break the strike completely, but Rogers had his own fleet on English Bay with an equally aggressive plan to shut down fishing.

The gillnet fleet at work off Steveston in 1900. Thousands of fishers worked in close quarters on the treacherous shoal waters of the Fraser River's estuary. RICHARD HENRY TRUEMAN PHOTO, CITY OF VANCOUVER ARCHIVES, AM1589–: CVA 2 - 149

Steveston, seen here in 1908, was a quiet place in the off-season but roared to life when the salmon ran. Accessible only by steamer or a day-long stage trip from Vancouver, it was effectively unorganized territory, ruled by the canning companies in their own interests. PHILIP T. TIMMS PHOTO, CITY OF VANCOUVER ARCHIVES, AM54-S4–: OUT P676.2

Nikkei fishers, afflicted by typhus and fever in their crowded, smoky bunkhouses, raised the funds to build the Steveston Japanese Hospital, open to people of all races. A secret payment made by the canners to pay off the hospital's debt was a factor in Nikkei fishers' decision to end their strike. CITY OF VANCOUVER ARCHIVES, AM54-S4-: OUT P689

Yasushi Yamazaki, seen here sitting with a baby on his lap, surrounded by family and *Tairiku Nippo* reporters, was picked to lead the Nikkei fishers because of his fluent English, two-fisted style and bargaining skills. He went on to become one of the Nikkei community's most influential leaders, in part as editor of *Tairiku Nippo* (the *Continental Times*). NIKKEI NATIONAL MUSEUM. 2001.11.33

Port Essington, located at the mouth of the Ecstall River on the south shore of the Skeena, was Steveston's northern counterpart, a turbulent boardwalk town owned by a former missionary where Tsimshian, Nikkei and fishers from every corner of the British Empire gathered for the salmon harvest. Yasushi Yamazaki and George Kelly both passed through Port Essington in the years before their encounter on the Fraser. W. R. LORD PHOTO, CITY OF VANCOUVER ARCHIVES, AM54-S4-: OUT P343

The Port Simpson waterfront in 1900, a unique amalgam of European-style housing and the totems emblematic of Tsimshian culture and society. George Kelly lived between this world and the English colonial homes of Victoria. IMAGE F-04470 COURTESY OF THE ROYAL BC MUSEUM AND ARCHIVES

Elizabeth Diex, photographed in about 1869, had been married early in life to a Quebecois Hudson Bay employee in Port Simpson, but found her way to Victoria where she became a domestic servant in the homes of the city's elite. A Tsimshian matriarch, she was George Kelly's adoptive mother and played a critical role in the community naming him Lige'ex, one of the most important names in the Tsimshian world. IMAGE ZZ-95324 COURTESY OF THE ROYAL BC MUSEUM AND ARCHIVES

The Port Simpson brass band leads a funeral procession in 1907 across the causeway linking the main community with Rose Island. Music and brass bands were an integral element of community life, a new expression of Tsimshian leadership and Indigenous culture in the context of colonialism and missionary control. IMAGE B-03958 COURTESY OF THE ROYAL BC MUSEUM AND ARCHIVES

Building cans in a Fraser River cannery in the late 1890s: men, women and children of all races worked long hours when the salmon ran. As contract labour, they were paid by the can or the case, seeing their wages whittled away by deductions for food, board and other necessities. NORMAN CAPLE PHOTO, CITY OF VANCOUVER ARCHIVES, AM54-S4-: SGN 1466

When the salmon runs began in earnest, the canners took every possible fish, but when cannery crews were overwhelmed, they imposed daily catch limits on each boat and slashed prices. In 1900, fishermen attempted to force both higher prices and higher daily limits. LEONARD FRANK PHOTO, VANCOUVER PUBLIC LIBRARY 15323

The Fraser gillnetters were strictly work boats, with no concession whatsoever to crew comfort or safety. The Nikkei fishermen delivering this heavy load could only manoeuvre against wind and tide with long oars, a back-breaking job. IMAGE B-08416 COURTESY OF THE ROYAL BC MUSEUM AND ARCHIVES

Union strikers march down the Steveston dyke, probably on their way to confront Nikkei fishers they believed might be ready to sign with the canners. Throughout the strike, some Nikkei fishers remained strong union supporters. LIBRARY AND ARCHIVES CANADA/HENRY JOSEPH WOODSIDE FONDS/A016346

Union fishermen rally in the fields behind the canneries, probably conducting the strike vote that ensured the strike continued after Nikkei fishers settled in 1900. Barely visible in the distance are three men gathered on a stage, perhaps Rogers and the two Indigenous union supporters who conducted the vote. LIBRARY AND ARCHIVES CANADA/HENRY JOSEPH WOODSIDE FONDS/A017205

Union fishermen march down the Steveston dykes in a show of strength designed to intimidate the canners and to impress any wavering Nikkei fishers. These demonstrations and counter marches by Nikkei fishermen convinced the canners they needed military assistance to break the strike. LIBRARY AND ARCHIVES CANADA/ HENRY JOSEPH WOODSIDE FONDS/A017207

Henry Bell-Irving, owner of ABC Packing Co., was the most powerful of the salmon canners in 1900 and coordinated their efforts to break the strike. IMAGE COURTESY OF THE BELL-IRVING FAMILY

Members of the Sockeye Fusiliers, the brims of their straw hats pinned up with tin stars cut from salmon cans, relax in Steveston, with Lieutenant Colonel Worsnop front and centre. CITY OF VANCOUVER ARCHIVES, AM54-S4-: MIL P184.2

The Duke of Connaught's Own Rifles regiment prepares to set up camp behind Malcolm and Windsor's Gulf of Georgia cannery. The pillbox hats were useless against the summer sun and were soon replaced. LIBRARY AND ARCHIVES CANADA/ HENRY JOSEPH WOODSIDE FONDS/A017203

The Nikkei fleet, flying Rising Sun flags, heads to the grounds in the wake of Dantai's settlement and the arrival of the militia. This apparent victory for the canners failed to end the strike. CITY OF VANCOUVER ARCHIVES, AM54-S4-2-: CVA 371-148

Photographer H. J. Woodside had a very limited stock of negatives with him in Steveston during the 1900 strike, so why use one for this group of "strikers," some in suits, some in work clothes? Union leaders meeting reporters? Frank Rogers in discussions with canners? We don't know. LIBRARY AND ARCHIVES CANADA/HENRY JOSEPH WOODSIDE FONDS/A017201

The salmon fleet sets sail in the wake of the final union settlement in 1900. LIBRARY AND ARCHIVES CANADA/HENRY JOSEPH WOODSIDE FONDS/A017199

A Tsimshian chief in full regalia marches in Vancouver's 1900 Labour Day parade. The Tsimshian, although just one of the First Nations that formed a union local, was at the forefront of the strikes in 1900 and 1901, assisting with fundraising and the union's campaign for public support. CITY OF VANCOUVER ARCHIVES, AM54-S4-2-: CVA 371-1156.4

The Nelson's Cornet Band, now in full Tsimshian regalia, marches in the 1900 Vancouver Labour Day parade in the 500 block of West Hastings. Indigenous leaders hoped their participation in the union would assist their effort to avoid displacement by the Nikkei, but their hopes were to be disappointed. JOHN TYSON PHOTO, CITY OF VANCOUVER ARCHIVES, AM54-S4-: IN P120.1

With the strike's end in 1900, the fleet went to work in earnest with substantially higher prices than the canners had hoped to pay. But the divisions revealed by the conflict were carefully exploited by the canners to achieve a much different outcome a year later. EDWARD BROS. PHOTO, CITY OF VANCOUVER ARCHIVES, AM54-S4-: IN P24

Nelson's Cornet Band, ready for a command performance for the Duke and Duchess of Cornwall in 1901. Only one of the ensemble is wearing a mask: George Kelly, lower left. EDWARD BROS. PHOTO, CITY OF VANCOUVER ARCHIVES, AM54-S4-: IN P24

CHAPTER 8

THE STORM

Strong southeasterly winds were beginning to whip the waters of the Strait of Georgia by the afternoon of July 10, driving the gillnetters off Point Grey closer to English Bay and the city, or deeper into the North Arm of the Fraser. The Nikkei fleet had been warned not to fish at night. Fear of violence, as well as the rising storm, had already forced most of the fleet back to Steveston. As Yamazaki ran deeper into English Bay, his miserably seasick police officers huddling under a tarpaulin, the lookout heard voices shouting in English.

The *Albion* quickly came upon a union boat "with ten white and one black fisherman ... threatening us with guns and curses. Suddenly, [our] two huge policemen appeared from their hiding places and showed their guns," Yamazaki recalled years later. "The men were shocked. We tied them up, one by one, landed at English Bay, and brought them to the Vancouver Police Station, three miles away. It had been like rounding up a herd of cows!"

The *Province*'s version told of two police officers lying in the bottom of a Japanese gillnetter, undoubtedly one of Yamazaki's fleet, and springing from concealment with pistols in hand to arrest six BCFU supporters. By 2 a.m., the union men were marched through the quiet streets of Vancouver, handcuffed and guarded by police with drawn pistols, to the Vancouver lockup. Those charged were two Chileans or Filipinos, R. Opeaga and Louis Luddon; Charles Forrest, a West Indian; and three "Europeans," Charles Walleck (or Willig), G. Gullivan and W. Wellington. Police seized shotguns, rifles and pistols from the union boat.[155]

There was mute evidence of other clashes floating in the waters of English Bay. The *Gabriola*, a fishing steamer out of Victoria, came upon an upturned boat off Point Atkinson, its mast broken and holes punched through the floorboards on either side of the bow. There was no sign of the crew. Other ships returning to English Bay told of hearing gunfire. Yamazaki resumed the search for the seven missing Nikkei fishermen, scanning the north shore of English Bay and then working west. As the sky lightened, the *Albion* encountered the tug *Defiance*, with a large log boom in tow, heading for First Narrows. On board were another seven Nikkei fishermen who told a harrowing tale. Yamazaki had not been the only one hunting fishermen on English Bay.

The Nikkei men told of setting off in several boats on July 10 from Imperial Cannery in Steveston. They worked their way north to Point Grey, where they set their nets to intercept sockeye heading into the North Arm. The wind began to blow, whipping up choppy seas, but that was the least of their problems. A blue ship with a black funnel, towing at least ten smaller boats, steamed out of English Bay, heading straight for them. Once off Point Grey, the smaller boats dropped off the tow line one by one. The Nikkei fishermen in their heavy Columbia River skiffs, with a single gaff-rigged sail and cumbersome oars, were powerless to escape any powered boat, especially when their nets were out. Ichitaro Suetsugu, Junjiro Nishizaki and three others were quickly set upon and "threatened with clubs and pistols." Three fishermen who had gone ashore to cook a meal fled into the bush, chased on their way by rifle fire from the pickets. Suetsugu and other fishermen nearby quickly surrendered. The union men slashed the nets to pieces, dragged the Nikkei into the patrol boat and headed for Bowen Island with the Nikkei boats in tow.

Once at Bowen, the union men forced the Nikkei ashore at gunpoint on a deserted beach with a small amount of food. They stripped their boats of oars, sails and rudders, warned them they would be killed if they resumed fishing and abandoned them. At dawn, the stranded Nikkei saw an overturned skiff floating near the beach with two of their countrymen clinging to its hull. Using crude paddles fashioned from flotsam and jetsam to propel themselves, they rescued the two and brought them to shore. Then the *Defiance* rescued them all from the beach for a two-dollar fee.[156]

By the time the Nikkei were safely aboard *Albion*, the early edition of the *Province* was on the streets with a sensational exclusive: seven Japanese fishermen had been kidnapped by union pickets and stranded on a secret island, where they would remain for the duration of the strike. Under the arresting headline "Captive Japs Spirited Away," the paper reported as many as twenty Nikkei had been taken prisoner. Citing a first-person account from an unnamed source, reporter R.W. Brown wrote that union leaders "say they will continue to maroon the Nikkei fishermen for the remainder of the season, or until the place is discovered by the authorities ... the Japs will be given food every few days and maintained comfortably, although closely guarded until a settlement is arrived at—that is the official statement of the fishermen this morning."[157]

The union fishermen did not wish to be misunderstood: "Individually we do not have any particular feelings of animosity against the Japs, and provided they don't hurt us in our trying to stop them from fishing, we won't do them any bodily harm. We will simply leave them on the little island." If there was gunfire, the spokesman said, it was because the Japanese fired first. If the Japanese were fishing, the union patrol simply "approached and with as little fighting as possible moved the Japs into their own boat, and after throwing overboard rifles and other firearms belonging to the Japs, turn the boat adrift."

In one case, the interviewed union man conceded, things had not gone smoothly. At 1:30 a.m. a Nikkei crew with its net out had fired at an approaching patrol boat. The pickets awaited a second boat for assistance and "we closed in and boarded their boat, having to take hold of the Japs and fight hand to hand with them. The sea was rolling very heavily and things all through were very precarious. We took pains not to hurt any of them. Very strict orders had been given that none of the Japs were to be hurt, unless they fired first and wounded some of the union men. I think that these instructions were obeyed to the letter, for not one was injured, although some shots were fired." Where was the island? Somewhere between Vancouver and Nanaimo, the source admitted, and the kidnapped Nikkei would be given "some grub every few days" and have a "pleasant little holiday safely out of the way from all further trouble until hostilities ended."

The *Province* exclusive was far too detailed for the union leadership's liking. The BCFU executive issued a statement "to give their official denial to the harmful and highly coloured sensational descriptions of unlawful acts alleged to have been committed by union patrol boats. It is emphatically denied that any union fishermen gave out such accounts of methods adopted to destroy Japanese boats as have been published."[158] This denial would prove an embarrassment.

A follow-up report in a later edition of the *Province* claimed thirty-six Japanese fishermen had been marooned, but persistent reports of two missing Japanese fishermen raised the more disturbing possibility that picket-line strife had escalated to manslaughter or even murder. The likelihood of anyone, even a strong swimmer, surviving more than thirty minutes in the Strait of Georgia was exceedingly low, but the wind and waves that had lashed the approaches to the Fraser that night made it impossible to know if missing fishermen had been lost to the storm or to violence. No union fishermen were reported missing. At least two Nikkei were unaccounted for, however, and their fate never determined.

By morning, Yamazaki had returned the marooned men to Vancouver. Now he executed a masterstroke that effectively ended the strike. The arrested union men were to be charged in open court on Friday, July 12. BCFU supporters, many reportedly carrying firearms, headed to court just before noon. After consultation with the police, Yamazaki struck on a plan to take his rescued fishermen to the court as well. With luck, they would be able to identify their kidnappers in the courtroom audience.

A large crowd of strikers had gathered on Hastings Street to watch the prisoners' arrival, in an atmosphere the *World* reporter thought as ominous as the moments before a thunderstorm. There were grumblings and protests as the arrested fishermen were marched into court, manacled in pairs. Proceedings were delayed while police urged the judge, H.O. Alexander, to order a general search for firearms. He wisely refused, alert to the confrontation that might result. The charges faced by the union men were very serious, ranging from kidnapping to possession of concealed firearms, but they were soon overshadowed by the arrival of the Nikkei.[159]

Striding into the crowded courtroom, Yamazaki's men quickly found their target, identifying Rogers as one of their assailants, as well as Joe Desplaines, another union supporter. Rogers was short, slender, with "fair mustaches, a dark soft hat" and had worn a long dark overcoat that night. Rogers was the "boss man," they testified later, but carried no firearms. Yamazaki later provided a colourful but only partly true account of the dramatic encounter in court:

> It was a strange scene we wouldn't have expected to see in a Japanese court. The first person to be identified was CPR harbour worker Rogers, a known face as the leader of many strikes. Japanese fishermen cried, "It's him! He was wearing a black coat that night," then he was sent to a basement room. A few more white men were identified and they were also sent down to the basement. However, most people in the gallery were white fishermen, or their sympathizers and they made a huge stink, creating turmoil in the court.
>
> They hurled abuse at the judge, saying, "This guy is partial to Japanese fishermen. We can't have a fair judgement with him." Not only that, someone shot at the judge and everyone in the gallery rushed to the exits. They ran like baby spiders running from their nest, with the police chasing after them. Even the

judge, young Mr. Taylor, rose from his seat and joined in the police chase. The courtroom, which should have been quiet, was a scene of complete anarchy.

In fact, Rogers and Desplaines surrendered quietly, were searched and taken to a cell. No shots were fired. Within hours, they were back in court entering "not guilty" pleas to a sweeping set of charges. As Alexander committed Rogers and Desplaines for trial without bail, police magistrate J.A. Russell offered a procedural suggestion to prosecutor William Bowser that drew a strong objection from J.H. Senkler, the union lawyer. The fishermen in court loudly cheered Senkler on. Russell, after all, had personal connections to the canners and had hired his own steam tug to conduct illegal searches of union pickets. Alexander ordered the courtroom cleared of everyone except lawyers, the accused and members of the press. Even Russell was sent packing.

Just minutes later and a few blocks away, Russell was accosted by Michael Sullivan, a BCFU member who had just emerged from a bar. He had seen Russell on the grounds, Sullivan said. "I had a bead on you and you had a lucky escape. If you had stayed out a little longer you would have carried some lead in your skull." In fact, he continued, "I've got a good notion to put a bullet through you now," and reached for his pocket. Russell shouted for help and tried to arrest Sullivan, but the drunken fisherman broke loose, ran east and disappeared down a passageway between the Granville Hotel and the Terminus Saloon. It was a tragicomic conclusion to a catastrophic day for the BC Fishermen's Union.[160]

The violence seemed to eliminate any prospects of unity, but reports from Steveston told a very different story. By midday July 11, as the union pickets closed in on the Nikkei fishermen off Point Grey, more than one thousand Nikkei boats were scattered across the waters at the mouth of the Fraser and the North Arm. In late afternoon, as the weather changed, driving rain pounded down on the fleet and the wind began to blow hard from the west. Most of the Nikkei fleet quickly found safety back in Steveston, but even here there was little shelter. The rising winds and waves caused havoc along the dykes, where First Nations canoes were battered against the rocks. Nikkei fishermen rushed to help.

"The yelling of the Indians, as they tried to get their boats back into position or bring them over the dyke, could be heard all over Steveston," one reporter wrote. "It is a well-known fact that there is no love lost between the Indian and the Jap, but it may be said to the personal credit of the latter that they never lost a moment in going to the assistance of the Indians. To hear an Indian boss a Jap, even in English so broken that it is falling to pieces, is worth listening to." As the fishermen sought to minimize the chaos—dozens of canoes were damaged or destroyed—"lightning was playing a tattoo along the horizon." The deep divisions of the strike were momentarily washed away in the rain and wind. In the face of the storm, First Nations and Nikkei fishermen found the common ground that otherwise eluded them.[161]

Rogers was again in jail, facing a range of serious charges. This time there would be no quick release, no bail. Rumours of a split in the Nikkei fleet that would result in many joining the strike proved false. A meeting of several hundred Nikkei fishermen July 12 in front of the hospital was tumultuous, but reporters in Steveston could not understand a word that was said. Kamekichi Ohki had been expelled from the gathering—or had he walked out? In any case, the Nikkei prepared to fish in even greater numbers. Yamazaki's protection was proving effective.

A dispirited gathering of the BCFU's Grand Lodge that night in Vancouver organized relief for the families of those in jail, issued renewed complaints about false naturalization papers and adjourned quietly. Any basis for unity between union fishermen and the Nikkei, fractured by the price settlements in 1900, had ended with the battle in English Bay. Two days later, the two Nikkei fishermen were still missing and feared dead.[162]

In the preliminary hearing on July 14, several Nikkei witnesses identified Rogers as the leader of the kidnapping conspiracy. Nikkei and white fishermen jostled and insulted each other in court. One fisherman, Osaki, told the court how he and a fellow fisherman had been accosted by a picket boat off Point Grey and detained while the union men consulted the "boss man," whom he identified in court as Rogers. Rogers arrived in a second boat, searched their gillnetter for firearms and then directed the union men not to cut the Nikkei fishers' net because there was no evidence they had been fishing. They were nonetheless taken to Bowen, where they were stranded with their boats, but without oarlocks, oars or sails.[163]

Then Rogers's situation, already grim, quickly worsened. Bowser subpoenaed *Province* reporter R.W. Brown to the stand and pressed him to name the source for his exclusive interview on the kidnapping of the Nikkei fishermen, which had proved uncannily accurate. Despite the union lawyer's objections, Bowser won agreement from the judge that a reporter's commitment to keep a source off the record was not privileged. In that case, Bowser declared, a continued refusal to answer would be contempt of court, punishable by imprisonment for eight days and then indefinite detention until the question was answered. Alexander agreed, adding that he would deny bail to all the fishermen and hold all of them in prison until he got an answer.

At that Brown crumbled. The source, he admitted, was Rogers himself. It was Rogers who had declared that union fishermen would now be armed. The reporter's humiliation was just beginning. He produced a written statement, signed by Rogers, that had been carried in the paper almost unaltered. Rogers and the *Province* reporter had clearly enjoyed a close and mutually beneficial relationship. Rogers had not said he was present for the kidnapping, Brown protested, but he could not deny that his scoop had exact details that could only be known to a participant. Bail was denied.[164]

Rogers's arrest signalled a new and critical stage in the strike, as it had in 1900. This time, however, with Rogers in prison facing a lengthy jail term, the union fishermen desperately sought a route to settlement. According to George Mackie, president of the New Westminster local, the issue was coming down to whether "Japanese and other aliens, or the British fishermen should control the fishery ... There did not seem to be any alternative 'except that of giving up the fish to the Japs and leaving the country or fighting for [our] rights against a horde of foreigners protected by our own police.'"[165] A major fishermen's meeting held in Vancouver July 15, chaired by Socialist party leader Ernest Burns, now apparently the president of the BCFU, had a strong anti-Asiatic tone. The possibility of unity across race lines, if it had ever existed, had disappeared in battles on English Bay.[166]

On July 19, the BCFU agreed to a price: 12.5 cents a fish for the season, no limits, for the first 25 percent of the pack, with the price declining to 10 cents thereafter. Calculation of the total pack and the final price was in the hands of the canners. The fishermen had capitulated. No one suggested, as they had in 1900, that this exceeded the Nikkei settlement. This was a complete victory for the canners, ratified by a unanimous vote of the union fishermen after a mediation session conducted by a panel of eminent Vancouver busi-nessmen. There is no record of the views of First Nations leaders, but the Tsimshian had once again been true to their word, refusing even to move to Steveston until a settlement was in place. On the morning of July 20, several hundred Port Simpson residents hurriedly packed up their camp in Vancouver by the Evans, Coleman and Evans wharf and headed to the Fraser. By now, the first flush of the run was arriving off Sand Heads, the arriving schools of sockeye visible from the cannery wharves. The tensions of the strike were submerged in a tidal wave of sockeye.[167]

The Big Year run that followed broke all records. The pace of production was so brutal that Chinese cannery workers struck on several occasions, in one case holding a foreman at knifepoint until he rehired two men terminated for sloppy work. In mid-August, the waste from the canneries was carried by the river and tide around Point Grey into English Bay. The steamer *Surrey* had "more difficulty in pushing her way through the mass of salmon running the river than she had in the ice floes of last winter." Thousands of salmon, surplus to the canners' requirements, were thrown away. The smell of rotting sockeye on city beaches was unbearable, in Steveston even worse.[168]

More than a century later, the records of the International Pacific Salmon Fisheries Commission would confirm that the 1901 run was the largest ever recorded at forty million fish, ten times the four million sockeye estimated to have returned in 1900. Once the Big Year run began, it is doubtful that any union, regardless of its structure, could have held the fishermen at the dock. In the face of that reality, it is not surprising that Rogers's efforts proved unsuccessful, but it's a tribute to the determination of the fishermen that they fought as long as they did.

Rogers languished in the Vancouver jail, out of the news but much in his membership's mind. His dream of organizing workers across racial lines was in ruins. The union, now under Charles Durham's leadership, met in convention on September 26 and 27 in New Westminster. Although in favour of seine fishing west of Saturna Island, the southernmost of the Gulf Islands in Canadian territorial waters, the union men advised the fisheries minister by telegram that "there is no doubt in our mind that the introduction of trap fishing in our province will totally destroy the means we fishermen have of earning a living." The fishermen felt their future slipping away.

By 1902, First Nations fishers would find themselves facing the guns of Nikkei pickets who wanted to strike for a better deal. By then, it was far too late to rebuild the fragile connection created in 1900. A petition to Queen Victoria from a First Nations chief seeking relief from Nikkei encroachment on the Fraser was simply filed away with the notation "no action." A subsequent appeal from Chief Harry Squamish, Chief Tom Mission, Chief Joe Capilano and elders of bands at False Creek, Musqueam, New Westminster and Point Roberts requested help to achieve a "settled price" as well as action against the Nikkei who "work for such little pay that we have no chance to make a living." It met a similar fate.[169]

On September 30, 1901, the Duke and Duchess of Cornwall arrived in Vancouver by private railcar to inaugurate the Duke of Connaught's Own Rifles drill hall on Beatty Street, an imposing brick pile capped with parapets carved from Gabriola limestone. Most of the DCOR volunteers were back from the Boer War, although some remained with Empire forces tracking down the last of the Boers' guerrilla forces. Their duties done, the Royals were saluted on their departure by a triple honour guard of DCOR men, a naval detachment from HMS *Warspite* and "Indian braves from Port Simpson." It was the Nelson's Cornet Band, including George Kelly, all in distinctive regalia made for the occasion, marching with the militiamen who had been mobilized to end their strike the summer before.

Rogers finally went to trial October 11 on the kidnapping charges. He pleaded not guilty. He had been present that night, he conceded, but denied all the evidence of his Nikkei accusers, insisting he had never counselled violence, had not been involved in the "kidnap," and had only heard of the confrontation off Point Grey second-hand. He acknowledged talking to *Province* reporter R.W. Brown, but said he had been badly misquoted. Brown pleaded guilty to exaggeration, but his story and his testimony became the prosecution's main weapon. To the outrage of prosecutor William Bowser, the jury acquitted Rogers after a brief deliberation. Thirteen unions had contributed $234.50 to Rogers's defence.

Bowser had proceeded only on some of the charges. Police inspector Colin Campbell quickly filed an affidavit citing conversations he had overheard among jurors indicating a firm bias for the fishermen. Declaring bitterly that the prosecution could not get a fair trial in union-friendly Vancouver, Bowser immediately appealed. Rogers and Desplaines, now in manacles, were denied bail and transferred to New Westminster to be tried a second time.

The New Westminster jury was sworn in on October 21 and the trial began October 29. The case was argued in a day. Slowly the prosecution's case unravelled. Eventually Rogers's lawyer made a direct appeal to the jury's racial prejudices. Who would they believe, he asked, the white fishermen or the "aliens"? Bowser conceded the point. If the jury accepted the Nikkei testimony, they could convict on it alone, he said.

If they preferred a "white" source, they could rely instead on the *Province* report and convict on that basis. On October 30, the foreman reported the jury could not come to a verdict. Rogers and his co-accused had been acquitted again.

Still Bowser would not give up, releasing the other union men but holding Rogers in prison for a third trial that could not be heard until the spring assizes of 1902. Rogers's applications for bail had been rejected three times by three different judges. On November 19, nearly three weeks after the verdict, Bowser finally relented, recommending the union leader be released on commitment of $2,000 bail plus $2,000 in securities. One of the socialist's guarantors was Charles Woodward, owner of the increasingly successful department store at Hastings and Abbott.[170]

Rogers was reluctant to talk to a waiting *World* reporter when he finally walked out of the New Westminster jail: "Brown and his scoop got me in trouble enough." He was noticeably thin. "I have no flesh on me at all." He showed the reporter "the wrist of a candidate for Kamloops air," a reference to the province's tuberculosis sanatorium. Had Rogers become infected in the damp jail? It was possible, although the labour movement had ensured he had ample food and he received regular visits, including one from MacLain. His hat pulled down, the collar of his long coat turned up, Rogers remained "keen of speech," but uninterested in an interview. He was headed for a hunting trip before returning to work, he said, then walked away.[171]

On December 17, 1901, the Privy Council released its decision in the Homma case. Eberts had thrown everything possible into the mix, warning that the Asiatics in BC—then about twelve thousand Nikkei and Chinese males—was enough to tip the balance of power and wrest control away from the white male population. Vote-buying would become rampant and Asian men would have access to a right not accorded to white women, which was clearly unthinkable. The best solution, he argued, would be to keep the Nikkei without the vote, lest a decision to extend the franchise ultimately benefitted women and Indigenous people. To the dismay of the Nikkei, Eberts was successful. Citing a strange US precedent, the court in London overturned the Canadian judges and upheld BC's right to limit the franchise. The defeat also meant that Asians were barred from numerous jobs available only to voters, including hand-logging or operating a pharmacy, since the electors' list was maintained by the province. The defeat suffered by the Nikkei would also affect Indo-Canadians, the Chinese and First Nations.[172]

On September 30, 1901, the *Vancouver Daily World* celebrated the visit of the Duke and Duchess of York with a dramatic banner headline: "Welcome to the West: Our Future King and Queen Receive the Homage of this Magic City." The Boer War veterans received medals, thousands lined the streets and "Red Men"—the Nelson's Cornet Band in Tsimshian regalia—"eloquently expressed their loyalty." A feature of the evening entertainment, as the ducal party dined on the *Empress of India*, was the illumination of the fishing fleet.[173]

Since 1899, British Columbia had been in turmoil, politically and economically. Elections had been inconclusive, critical industries crippled by strikes. Newcomers had demanded the right to vote. British Columbia's soldiers had travelled to the other side of the earth to uphold a colonial system that had disappeared in their own province a generation before. Nearly one in ten of them was killed or injured. Now new currents were gaining strength in Victoria, where another election was imminent. A consensus was emerging to fight the next election along party lines, to eliminate the turmoil in the legislature. The strike wave was abating. The soldiers were home. The wave of Nikkei immigrants had abated. Slowly but surely, life was returning to the established order.

CHAPTER 9

AFTERMATH

The Boer War had been won, the Big Year run had returned in staggering abundance, but many touched by the turmoil of those years had little to celebrate. Among the DCOR's South Africa veterans were some who wished they had "left their bones in the land of the Boers," who found survival worse than death. One was New Westminster's Corporal A.O. Lohman: a violin maker, veteran of the German Imperial Army and an employee of the provincial asylum. Only thirty years old when he volunteered for the Boer campaign, he had been riddled with nine bullets in the first charge at Paardeberg. He survived, haunted by hearing the sound of his own blood dripping in puddles on the casualty centre floor. In January 1903, by then a member of the British Columbia Police, he was caught cashing a fraudulent cheque. In debt, depressed, alcoholic, unable to accept that he had lived when others had died, he shot himself with his own revolver. "Why was I not killed in the last battle in South

Africa?" his suicide note read. "I would then have died an honourable death."[174]

Bell-Irving found that the defeat of the BCFU, aided in part by the DCOR's Sockeye Fusiliers, was not enough to save the canners from financial disaster. Despite his careful preparations and the massive catches, the 1901 salmon season ended with a wave of bankruptcies. This was of little concern to Bell-Irving personally; ABC Packing was vertically integrated, well financed, carefully managed and exceedingly profitable. Bell-Irving felt ready to weather any storm. Now only forty-four and at the peak of his career, he was prepared to leave the battles of the fishing industry to others, preferring to relax on his yacht or travel to England, where his boys were enrolled in exclusive private schools. So he did.[175]

The other canners were not so secure. The huge fleets of gillnetters had driven up costs. The enormous pack of 1901 flooded the market and drove down prices. Even though BC canners had paid only 10 and ⅝ cents a fish on average, their American counterparts had paid even less. A young twenty-seven-year-old American named Henry Doyle, who had learned the inner workings of the canning industry by selling linen gillnet twine, secured the backing of a Bay Street stock promoter to acquire options on thirty-four companies owning forty-two canneries, the majority on the Fraser. Bell-Irving refused to sell, but canner Alexander Ewen, a founder of the industry, agreed to become the new firm's president, adding instant credibility. Doyle launched the BC Packers Association on May 20, 1902, quickly shutting down seven Fraser canneries for good. The closures, combined with widespread investment in automated equipment, cut hundreds of jobs ashore and afloat.[176]

Although the union had held the line on prices in 1900 and survived with an agreement in 1901, it emerged from the Big Year divided and adrift. Like A.O. Lohman, Rogers struggled to rebound from the battles of 1901, despite his ultimate acquittal. For a year after his release he remained out of sight, working as a longshoreman, absent from the reports of union or socialist gatherings, missing from the political rallies he had helped organize just two years earlier. The BCFU found new leadership, but the lessons of the strikes were straightforward to the rank and file: expulsion of the Nikkei was the only priority. Was this a direction Rogers would not go? There was certainly little room for racism on the waterfront, where men of every race, including the Squamish Nation's Bows and Arrows longshore crew, worked side by side.

In the 1902 negotiations, Durham and Watson led the union to a new agreement paying a sliding scale between eleven cents and twenty cents based on the size of the pack. This arrangement, vulnerable to manipulation throughout the season, gave the canners effective control of the price. The union then recommended that locals "be guided by temporary arrangements and their own judgement." Union recognition, of a sort, had at last been secured; the new price agreement was lost. The canners promised to deduct and remit union dues, the BCFU's version of the special hospital payment to the Nikkei.

The union settled first that year, determined to beat the Nikkei to a deal, and a union spokesman shrugged off criticism from First Nations chiefs with the suggestion they were "not quite capable of seeing through the intricacies." This time it was Nikkei fishers who drew guns in an effort to stop Indigenous gillnetters from setting their nets, but their attempted strike soon collapsed. The Nikkei, too, accepted a sliding scale and collective bargaining on the Fraser was effectively at an end. The canners' victory over the fishermen was complete. The clear racial lines drawn in those years would persist for a half century.

Then a new labour battle, the 1903 strike of the United Brotherhood of Railway Employees (UBRE) against the CPR, found Rogers once more on the picket line. The strike began February 27 when the CPR fired a clerk for union activities. The UBRE united freight handlers, warehousemen and general labourers, but not the craft unions—especially locomotive engineers and machinists—who kept the trains running. The information against the clerk had been gathered by the CPR's Special Services Department, a new internal security force organized to replace the Pinkerton and Thiel detectives who had fought unions since the railway's founding.

CPR managers were anxious to stop the spread of organization beyond the less skilled trades, and determined to eliminate the threat of job action on key spur lines to the mining districts. They decided to break the UBRE. Nonetheless, the job action soon paralyzed the CPR's western operations and began to impact the city's economy. What began as a strike by 154 workers quickly expanded to all the freight handlers on the Vancouver docks. Longshoremen unloading the CPR's *Empress of India* struck the ship March 4 and the job action closed the waterfront as CPR deckhands and telegraph messengers joined in. Soon one thousand workers across Western Canada were off the job, but the company refused to yield. A tentative settlement was rejected by the railway in early March. The CPR soon began importing strikebreakers and special police, armed thugs who lived in the retired sidewheeler steamer *Yosemite* at the dock near the north foot of Abbott Street.[177]

By mid-March, strikers had convinced Italian and Nikkei workers who had been imported to unload trains to respect the picket lines. The Western Federation of Miners struck the Dunsmuir mines, at least in part to cut off coal to CPR ships. A coal shortage loomed, so the labour council arranged for direct import of a barge of coal from Ladysmith for sale to the public with the proviso that none would be available to the CPR. But the determination of some skilled workers to continue working undermined the UBRE picketing. Craft union leaders ordered machinists and engineers to move the trains. A boycott of the CPR was the labour movement's response, and Rogers was among those who organized a sympathy strike of longshoremen as the strike intensified. Opposing this action was Joseph Watson, who had persuaded local boilermakers not to support the strike. Now union activists who had fought shoulder-to-shoulder against the canners found themselves on opposite sides of a railworkers' picket line. Despite the boycott, the tide began running against the UBRE, which had not been able to shut down the trains now ferrying special police and strike-breakers to Vancouver.[178]

That winter Rogers had begun to reappear in public life. On January 29, he was a featured speaker at a campaign rally at the Theatre Royal in support of R.G. Macpherson, a Liberal candidate in the upcoming federal by-election and an uncompromising advocate of Asiatic exclusion. The fact that Rogers was considered an important speaker was indicative of his continued influence. Evidently still a Socialist, he was moving closer to the mainstream of city politics. The diversity of those who stood bail for him was a testament to the respect he had won during the strike years.

The 1900 city voters' list had Rogers living at the "city slip" at the foot of Gore Avenue, likely on a boat. Rogers's world centred on a few square blocks of the waterfront from Hastings Mill to the train station. CPR's docks and rail yards were behind picket lines that lay only a few steps from the hotels, bars and outfitters' stores of Gastown, and a few blocks from the union offices and Socialist Party meeting rooms on Cambie and Westminster. Unlike the Steveston strikes, which had been fought on the Steveston dykes and the Strait of Georgia, the UBRE conflict was unfolding in the heart of the city. On Monday, April 13, 1903, Rogers had a late supper at Bill Williams's Social Oyster and Coffee House on Cordova Street just a few blocks from his home. It was after 11 p.m. when he stepped out onto the street with two friends and began walking east, perhaps toward his home at the foot of Gore.

The three men noticed a disturbance, they said later, near the Abbott Street rail crossing close to the *Yosemite* and Stimson's dock. There was a single gas light illuminating the tracks. As the three crossed the tracks, shots rang out—as many as eleven, according to one report. Rogers fell to his knees, downed by one of the first bullets. As soon as they could, Tom Sabatino and Larry O'Neill dragged him to safety, then to the Western Hotel and to the hospital just a few blocks away. It was clear the wound was likely to be fatal, but Rogers insisted on making a statement to Colin Campbell, the officer who had supervised policing of the 1900 strike and signed the affidavit that had forced Rogers to a second trial in 1901. Rogers's statement, corroborated by several witnesses, placed him at the scene as an innocent passerby. The text of his statement has not survived.

The shooting dominated the next day's papers. *The Daily World* reported that the CPR special officers had been aroused earlier that evening by an assault on one of their members. One claimed Rogers had been among those who beat the railway police officer. Yet another story recalled that Rogers had been mistaken on a previous occasion for a man named Tracy, another CPR special officer who protected strikebreakers. If so, had Rogers been shot by union supporters? It seemed far-fetched. Was he at the wrong place at the wrong time? Had the CPR special officers recognized Rogers under the light and seized their opportunity to kill him? Many thought so.

Rogers insisted he was strong enough to withstand the wound. Within twenty-four hours, however, he was in critical condition. No family members were reported at his bedside. Despite his conviction he would live, Rogers died at 3:30 p.m., Wednesday, April 15, 1903.

The bullet that killed Rogers was of small calibre, news reports speculated, but must have come from nearby. "It went through his overcoat and a stevedore's union constitution and bylaws book bound in a thick cardboard cover," according to one report, "and a thick card besides, and then through his coat, vest and underclothes." The bullet entered Rogers's abdomen on his right side, above the navel. The coroner later determined the cause of death was acute peritonitis, caused by his internal injuries. One .38-calibre bullet was recovered during the autopsy, but all agreed more shots were fired.

A CPR special officer who had boasted of shooting Rogers was quickly arrested and then released—his gun was the wrong calibre and had not been fired. Another suspect, CPR special officer James McGregor of Montreal, was then charged with the crime. The CPR's Vancouver lawyer conducted his defence. Two witnesses, O'Neill and Sabatino, testified that shots came both from near Stimson's office and from coal piles nearby. The first shots felled Rogers. Frank Armstrong, a CPR employee who had been working to protect the strikebreakers, testified that McGregor had acknowledged immediately after the incident that his bullets had found their mark: "I know that I shot someone. I saw him drop on one knee." Armstrong later changed his evidence to say he had heard no such thing. Others testified that there had been some kind of affray with strikers just minutes before the shooting incident, implying the shots were fired in self-defence.

The conflicting testimony suggested strikers and strike-breakers had clashed along the waterfront that night. CPR special officers hurried to the scene to assist their men. Rogers and his friends may have been coming to aid the strikers. Whatever had happened, both sides were on edge. There was no doubt about what happened next: gunfire from at least two locations, at least five shots in all, killed Rogers. Was Rogers targeted? Given his spontaneous decision to head to the tracks, it seems unlikely, but he was a familiar figure on the waterfront and was standing under a light. Nor was there any argument on another critical point: Rogers and his friends were unarmed.

After a short trial that began almost as soon as Rogers was interred, McGregor was acquitted by a jury. Apart from Armstrong's statement, quickly withdrawn, there was no evidence to connect him with the fatal bullet. According to reporters, he appeared utterly unafraid of conviction and moved into the audience rather than leave the court after he was discharged. The contrast with Rogers's legal ordeal on kidnapping charges could not have been starker.[179]

In the words of an "intimate friend" who gave the *World* a sketch of Rogers's life, "his was a daring soul, but he evidently was born under an ill-omened star, as he seemed to get into trouble very early—and on a number of cases innocently." In this account, Rogers was the "first lieutenant" to MacLain, when that "strong-minded, self-willed personage" took leadership of the strike. The friend recalled MacLain and Rogers taking the leaky launch *Starling* to Nanaimo to raise food and money for striking fishermen from the Nanaimo miners—in the teeth of a gale that had kept large steamers in port. The two were also in the same boat the night a fisherman, his nets out in defiance of the strike, threatened to blow Rogers's head off with a Winchester rifle. "This did not bother the unruffled Rogers. The substitute [scab] lost heart and the next minute his Winchester was at the bottom of the bay and he took a good many gulps of sea water before they placed him back in his boat and towed him in."

Quoting Shakespeare's Lady Macbeth, the friend concluded that "After life's fitful fever he sleeps well" would be an apt epitaph for Rogers's life and death. "Ill-omened star" and "life's fitful fever"—were these discreet references to a darker side of Rogers's personality? This friend clearly ranked MacLain above Rogers in the union's leadership, but that was not how the fishermen had seen it. It was Rogers, elected president in 1900, who remained in the front line in 1901, when MacLain's only contribution had been an attempt to bait the canners' special police into arresting him. MacLain had visited Rogers in prison, but the fact that labour's hero had been released from jail to meet a single reporter, then walked off alone—no family, no friends— underlines the mysteries that remain about one of the BC labour movement's most important figures.[180]

The funeral procession, one of the largest Vancouver had seen, drew hundreds of mourners, as many as fifteen hundred, according to one estimate. Socialist leader Ernest Burns, who had organized alongside Rogers during the events of 1900 and 1901, wrote years later that "about halfway to the end of the line of march a terrific storm burst, as cold and pitiless as capitalist justice itself." The march never faltered, and despite the pouring rain, "every head was bared."[181]

Delegations from every union—fishermen, postmen, railway workers, longshoremen and many others—marched in solemn procession to the grave at Mountainview Cemetery.

There was no mention of any family members, no pictures of labour's hero and no details in any tribute to Rogers of his life before the 1900 strike. The wreath on his grave read "martyr," and his fellow workers declared him one of the greatest leaders of their still-young movement, cut down at only thirty years of age. The granite headstone they later installed read: "Frank Rogers, Murdered by a Scab in Strike against CPR, Union Organizer and Socialist." It is impossible not to wonder who he really was—or who he might have become had he lived.

As Rogers was lowered into his Mountainview grave, George Kelly was being considered to assume the name Lige'ex, one of the most important titles in the Tsimshian world. His journey to this honour seems to have begun in 1901, when he moved to Port Simpson. Sometime during this period, Kelly met and married a woman named Alice Auroil, of Metlakatla, who was nearly twenty years his junior. The fate of his first marriage to Lucy Kelly, who bore him a daughter, Charlotte, and a son, George Jr., is unknown. In 1901, George Kelly and Alice Auroil (or Oriole) welcomed a daughter they named Elizabeth, no doubt named in tribute to his adoptive mother.[182]

Kelly's move north came as Tsimshian elders were wrestling with one of the most difficult decisions they had faced in many years. Ten years earlier, the sudden death of Paul Legaic II, the holder of the title Lige'ex, had precipitated a leadership crisis in the Gispaxlo'ots tribal group of the Tsimshian. Legaic II had lived for many years in Metlakatla under Duncan's authoritarian administration. His return to Port Simpson in the mid-1880s was celebrated with cannon salutes and a welcome ceremony that included fifty women dressed in marmot and marten skins. But Legaic's death in January 1891 left the Gispaxlo'ots with no obvious successor, a gap that Alfred Dudoward, chief of the Gitando, stepped forward to fill.

The Gispaxlo'ots and the Gitando vied with each other for the honour of committing Legaic's body to the grave, with the brass bands of the Riflemen and the Firemen competing for pride of place in the solemn procession to the cemetery. Secret preparations were undertaken by the Gispaxlo'ots, without informing the Gitando, to name Paul Legaic's niece Martha to the chieftaincy. Although the final commemorative feast to confirm Martha's ascendancy was held in December, Alfred Dudoward continued his efforts to become the supreme chief of the Port Simpson people. The struggle for the Lige'ex legacy continued in the form of arguments over the erection of a granite commemorative monument to the Lige'ex lineage, which would fulfill the role of a crest pole by listing all the men who had held the illustrious title.

Martha Legaic's ascendancy to the name proved a temporary solution. Only sixteen when she was appointed, she required the supervision of an elder to fulfill her obligations. She became increasingly independent, angering many Gispaxlo'ots by joining the Christian Band of Workers, committing herself to a Christian life. Although she recanted in 1902, she died unexpectedly on the Nass River in the same year, triggering a new period of controversy. Four elders were appointed to come up a solution. Chief Sgagweet, Alfred Dudoward, was ruled out. George Kelly was one possibility and Sarah Legaic, sister of Paul Legaic II, was another. Dudoward objected to her because she was a commoner. That left George Kelly, whose adoptive mother Diex had moved from the Gispaxlo'ots to the Gitando and who was himself a member of the house of Sgagweet, but a different branch. Naming him to the title offered the possibility of ending the rivalry once and for all. He moved to Port Simpson in 1902 but was not finally confirmed as Lige'ex until 1907. His mixed blood was no obstacle to his consideration.[183]

In an interview thirty years later with American ethnographer Viola Garfield, Kelly recounted how Diex had raised him in Victoria during her marriage to Lawson, and how he and his stepmother had returned to Lax Kw'alaams together in 1902. Diex set up a small store for the Gitando people. Soon after his arrival, Kelly took the name Ni'as we'bas, House of Sgagweet. Lige'ex's pole was ready to fall down; Diex decided to replace it with the stone monument, which is still standing in the village. It appears Kelly then moved to Metlakatla, where he was when Martha Legaic's death triggered a new succession crisis. A committee of chiefs, including Matthew Johnson, William Russ, Joseph Pierce and Henry Tate, asked Kelly to assume the name, telling him Alfred Dudoward and William Kelly had both refused. George Kelly refused as well, but the committee continued to press him, giving him a large dinner during the talks. Eventually, he agreed.[184]

When George Kelly arrived in Port Simpson to receive the name, the community fired rockets and blew whistles to mark his arrival. Missionary leaders of all denominations came down to the dock to greet him, and an interpreter was hired to translate the proceedings for them. The gathering concluded with three cheers for the new chief. Soon the chiefs of Kitkatla sent an invitation to Lige'ex to visit their community. Those who made the journey with Kelly found Kitkatla in the grip of a measles outbreak, but days of feasting and dancing followed to mark the arrival of the new Lige'ex.

Kelly's chieftainship would be hobbled both by his long childhood absence from Port Simpson and by his inability to live up to the financial and social obligations of leadership. As historian Peggy Brock writes, "Disease, low reproduction rates, alcohol abuse, violence and processed foods accompanied the imposition of a colonial state apparatus and the introduction of new religious and moral codes, and they, in turn, influenced the gradual eclipse of Lige'ex." Kelly may have had the leadership qualities necessary to bear his new responsibilities, but unlike Dudoward, who continued to operate a trading schooner and other enterprises, he had no financial clout. In a subsequent census, his occupation was listed as logger.[185]

In October 1901, before Kelly's departure for Port Simpson, the Nelson's Cornet Band marched once again through Vancouver's streets, this time at the centre of celebrations to welcome the visiting Duke and Duchess of Cornwall. Nearly every man had a *liu*, or cedar ring, around his neck, indicating his membership in a secret society. The Tsimshian chiefs presented the duchess with a ceremonial headdress or *amhalaayt*. Each band member was wearing a distinctive blanket decorated with Tsimshian crests over his dress suit. In a ceremonial photograph to mark the occasion, a rank of solemn archers stands with drawn bows behind the musicians, who are posed with their instruments. Chief Henry Nelson, resplendent in his own *amhalaayt*, sits with his saxophone in the front row. On his right sits George Kelly, his cloak draped over one shoulder, his dark shirt and light tie exposed. He is in the front rank but slightly apart, the only member of the band whose face is covered with a distinctive fitted mask, a conscious gesture that seems to insist "I am Tsimshian."[186]

Blind and infirm, Kelly died in Port Simpson on September 29, 1933 (according to the BC Death Index). He was seventy-six. The Lige'ex name has so far never been bestowed on a successor. Like Rogers, George Kelly was briefly well known, but in history his life remains largely a mystery.

Of all the groups that confronted the canners in 1900 and 1901, only the Nikkei counted themselves victors. For the first generation of Nikkei, Yamazaki was a central figure in the establishment of their community. As a friend put it, "The stakes were very high. If we'd lost, a few thousand Nikkei fishermen would all be doomed to unemployment and starvation. By winning the struggle, Nikkei fishermen could build a foundation for future development in Steveston. We owed a lot to Yamazaki for his devotion."[187]

But Yamazaki, true to form, did not rest on his laurels. He had many more careers ahead of him. He was brave, but not a fool. Life in Steveston would have been a dangerous undertaking given his direct involvement in the arrest of Rogers. By the winter of 1901, Yamazaki was back in Seattle editing a newspaper. He did not return to British Columbia permanently until 1908, although he operated a salt salmon export business to Japan from 1903 to 1906. In 1908, perhaps judging it safe to return, he accepted an appeal to take over *Tairiku Nippo (Continental Times)*, a struggling newspaper in Vancouver. Yamazaki had been recruited by a group of businessmen who needed his financial skills to raise the money necessary to stabilize the business. Yamazaki sought to move from the underworld of the Steveston docks to the Nikkei community's leadership, using his pen where he had once preferred a pistol or iron bar to make his point.

The paper, which had a wide circulation in the Nikkei community, flourished under Yamazaki's leadership, engaging in many intense controversies. Founded by a group of Buddhists, the *Tairiku* provided a key link for its readers to the wider world, particularly to the homeland. For many readers, even those who had never set foot in Japan or had immigrated to British Columbia fifteen or twenty years earlier, the *Tairiku* provided a perspective and worldview with Japan at its centre. Driven to the margins of Canadian life, the Nikkei could see themselves instead as part of the larger global Nikkei community, organized around the Emperor and the Yamato philosophy that emphasized the noble spirit of the Nikkei people. Yamazaki, as editor, was a proponent of this perspective. It was not assimilation he sought, it was equality. But for that, the Nikkei needed the vote, an objective that seemed beyond reach with Homma's defeat.[188]

Always the individualist, Yamazaki became a thorn in the side of the community's power brokers. An early muckraking campaign by Yamazaki exposed Nikkei involvement in the provision of prostitutes to brothels located along the CPR main line in Western Canada. The Japanese-language book that resulted from this series of exposés included an introduction from Vancouver's Chief Constable R.G. Chamberlain, who hailed the paper's willingness to tackle a problem that touched directly on the interests of substantial figures in the community. The *Tairiku* reports were written in clear, direct language that spared little; Yamazaki's reporter had interviewed the women themselves in "Tokyo Houses" in Nelson, Cranbrook and Alberta, naming names and publishing pictures. But among the Japanese themselves, writes historian Roy Ito, "no voices were raised to support Yamazaki's crusade. After all, prostitution was an accepted scheme of things in Japan where the needs of the Japanese male were pandered to without question." It was just one of a series of controversies that often put Yamazaki at odds with other community leaders.[189]

Despite continued growth and a measure of prosperity, the Nikkei community remained vulnerable. Community leaders did everything in their power to win the vote, but Vancouver's race riots of 1907, coming on the heels of years of anti-Asiatic agitation, showed how vulnerable they remained. (The Vancouver community was spared some of the destruction suffered in Chinatown by the organized defence provided by fishermen, who confronted the rioters along Gore Avenue and rained bricks on them from rooftops.)

With the outbreak of the First World War, Yamazaki saw an opportunity to unite the wider Nikkei community around a new strategy that he believed was bound to lead to the franchise. Armed forces recruiting offices that were set up in Vancouver in 1914 refused to accept Nikkei volunteers. In August 1914, with the war just weeks old, Yamazaki was in correspondence with the Canadian and Japanese authorities about his plan to overcome this prohibition as a precursor to winning the vote.[190] In the pages of his newspaper, Yamazaki urged Japanese men to volunteer for the war effort, using his leadership position in the Canadian Japanese Association to organize the recruits and begin training.

Despite the quick start, Yamazaki found the recruiting process lengthy, and resistance from the Canadian Army seemed unbreakable. By early 1915, however, one hundred Nikkei had volunteered and three times that many seemed a realistic goal. Regular drilling on the Powell Street Grounds was followed by marches to Stanley Park. In April 1915, however, trainees clashed with supporters of the *Canada Shimpo*, a rival newspaper critical of Yamazaki's efforts. The *Canada Shimpo* office was ransacked, and Yamazaki found himself fundraising to pay the fines of trainees charged in connection with the incident. Yamazaki's rival was unable to publish for two days. It was not the first time someone who challenged Yamazaki suffered violent repercussions.

The same month, in the wake of a fruitless twenty-day journey to Ottawa to appeal for the right to create a Japanese unit, Yamazaki was forced to disband his volunteers. The creation of a Japanese battalion had been categorically rejected in Ottawa. The volunteers cried and hugged at the dispersal ceremony, where the Canadian officer who had trained them gave them medals. Yamazaki told the men their only hope lay in Alberta, where Nikkei volunteers would be accepted if they applied as individuals, not an entire unit. They would have to pay their own way to Alberta, but they could go to war.

Yamazaki had expected to experience the glory of sending the troops to war, to enjoy the fame of becoming known in history as the organizer of the volunteer unit. "His voice trembled, his face crumpled and he cried in public for the one time in his life when he had to ask the men to pay their own way." Between thirty and forty soldiers made the trip to Calgary.[191]

Many of those men were killed or injured. Despite their sacrifices, Canada would never extend the franchise beyond those soldiers who fought in France. Yamazaki himself won the vote, perhaps as a consolation prize, without seeing combat. On January 8, 1916, he was among a group of "Canada's most prominent men" awarded naturalization under 1914 legislation that bestowed "empire-wide citizenship." Among others on the list were CPR president William Van Horne and Grand Trunk Railway president George Kelly, no relation to Chief Kelly of Port Simpson. Yamazaki retreated to his business interests, resigning from the leadership of the Canadian Japanese Association in 1917.

That summer he hosted four thousand community members to Hastings Park to celebrate the paper's tenth anniversary, lavishly catered with a program "along lines strictly 'Japanese'" that included geisha performances, dancing, bicycle races, baseball matches and much more. He maintained his financial interest in *Tairiku*, but his crusading fire seems to have sputtered out. He returned from Manchuria in 1920 in time to see the unveiling of the Stanley Park war memorial, commemorating the sacrifice of Japanese soldiers, then faded from public view. He died in obscurity in Japanese-occupied Manchuria, probably in 1941.[192]

Yamazaki was an individualist and an authoritarian. From his first lonely walk to Tokyo to his crusading days at the *Tairiku Nippo*, he showed what could be achieved with energy and determination, whether armed with a revolver or a pen. His goal of full equality for the Nikkei proved unattainable, but there is no indication that he ever had the slightest doubt that his actions were necessary and appropriate. He felt vindicated by the successes of the Nikkei community and its growing prosperity, never imagining the events that would lead to its wholesale destruction. But then, who would? Even those who championed Asiatic exclusion probably never expected that their dream would become reality in such decisive fashion.

On October 3, 1903, British Columbians went to the polls for the third time in five years to elect a provincial government. The outcome was a triumph for Richard McBride, the charming but combative New Westminster lawyer who had taken over the reins of the province's Conservatives.

McBride's imposition of party discipline ended the informal horse-trading among members of the legislature that had allowed Socialist MLAs like J.H. Hawthornthwaite, elected by the miners of Nanaimo, to win passage of the first Workmen's Compensation Act in Canada. During his first term, McBride won the support of Hawthornthwaite and Vancouver Island Socialist Parker Williams by permitting legislation to reduce working hours. In subsequent elections, however, McBride could safely ignore them. The Conservatives and the Liberals alternated in power for the next half century. The climate had been created, at last, for stable economic expansion.[193]

Only white men could vote in this reformed political system, which was based on strict racial segregation that had devastating economic consequences for Nikkei, Chinese and Indigenous citizens. Once the Privy Council decision upheld the rejection of Tomekichi Homma's application to vote, the provincial voters' list became the main weapon of Asiatic exclusion as industry after industry restricted access to voters only. With the victims of this policy unable to exercise legal or political pressure, no politician hesitated to play the race card. Homma's failed legal crusade for the right to vote, taken up in a different form by Yamazaki's First World War volunteers, set the stage for the progressive marginalization of the Nikkei people from economic life in the province, a process that culminated with the internment of the Nikkei in the wake of Pearl Harbor in 1942.

The expulsion of the Nikkei from the fishing industry resulted in confiscation of hundreds of boats from every section of the coast. Although most of the Nikkei boats were ultimately transferred to First Nations owners, it was too late for the First Nations fleet to regain its dominance. The combination of overfishing by American salmon traps and destruction of the main runs by the Hells Gate slide had reduced the Fraser to a minor producer in BC's salmon fishery.

First Nations had made acknowledgement of their land and Indigenous rights their priority, not winning the vote. Residential schools, continued economic marginalization and the depredations of the Department of Indian Affairs took a staggering toll. In 1920, in violation of repeated promises, Canada passed legislation authorizing cabinet to implement the recommendations of the McKenna–McBride Commission to reduce or cut off lands held by First Nations, whether or not they consented. Further legislation introduced by Arthur Meighen's Conservatives that year provided for "enfranchisement" for Indians, with or without consent, prohibiting "enfranchised Indians" from living on or being buried on reserves. This was followed by stronger government powers to take Indigenous children into custody and a renewed crackdown on potlatching, which resulted in jail terms for several chiefs.

Nonetheless, the Allied Tribes of BC continued to press for Indigenous rights and title until further legislation in 1927 made it illegal even to hire a lawyer to pursue a claim. With the collapse of the Allied Tribes, the chiefs of the Haida and Tsimshian First Nations convened in Port Simpson in 1931 to found the Native Brotherhood of British Columbia, an organization that would fight for fish prices as well as pursue other unspoken goals for the time being rendered illegal. (It is likely that Kelly, although in his twilight years, attended this gathering.) Their goal was equality, not assimilation. They favoured "retention of the native's identity, racially and culturally." This is a sentiment Yamazaki and other leaders of Dantai would have understood, even though exclusion of the Nikkei remained a key demand of First Nations leaders right up to the moment it happened.[194]

Were these racial divisions inevitable? The fevered cries for Asiatic exclusion, after all, reflected mainstream political opinion in 1900. Rogers's appeal to the Nikkei was as pragmatic as it was idealistic, driven by the desire to maximize unity against the canners. It was completely at odds with the virulent anti-Asiatic rhetoric that dominated the newspapers—and it worked. First Nations leaders would naturally have seen the white fishermen as their best allies, given the relatively recent arrival of the Nikkei on the scene, and their resentment of the Nikkei was obvious from Kelly's remarks.

But the Nikkei, too, saw the value of unity. They were determined to save their place in this new country and saw the negotiations as a chance to do so. Even if some "old-time Japs" wanted to stick with the union, it seems unlikely that hundreds of hungry young migrants who had arrived just months earlier would understand the strategic need for unity. Yet Yamazaki and his colleagues succeeded in holding them in line for weeks, even appealing to the union for food to sustain the dispute when rank-and-file pressure was growing irresistible. It was no doubt easier to keep the Nikkei fishermen in line with appeals to nationalist and racial pride than to any concept of union solidarity, but the Nikkei rank and file were educated men, well aware of the labour struggles underway in Japan.

Rogers's strategy proved effective, as the final settlement showed. The divisions along racial lines were real, but each section of the fleet reached across those barriers even after the economic pressure on the Nikkei became irresistible.

So the story of the Fraser strikes offers two glimpses of an alternative direction for British Columbia, a future in which people cooperated across racial lines because it made sense to do so. One came during that sunny July day on the field behind the Steveston canneries, where people of all races cast ballots under the careful monitoring of First Nations scrutineers. It was Rogers who collected those ballots, Rogers who attempted both in 1900 and 1901 to forge and maintain that link with the Nikkei. Working with him, despite their anger at the Nikkei, were the First Nations chiefs. The anger and resentment triggered by the Nikkei price settlement, an outcome the canners' achieved by mobilizing the militia, threatening starvation and offering special payment of community debts, was a turning point in the province's history, not just in the outcome of the dispute. From that day on, the Nikkei community leaders believed their place in this new land was secure, despite the losing forty-year battle they had to fight to maintain their place in the fishing industry.

The second glimpse of a different reality came a year later as the storm lashed the waters of the Fraser and the Strait of Georgia, threatening to destroy the canoes of the First Nations fishers right at the cannery docks. Overcoming their mutual fear and the barriers of language and culture, the Nikkei and Indigenous fishers rushed unquestioningly to the docks to save the First Nations canoes.

Both these events were occurring in a unique and short-lived world, isolated from the rest of the province, on the banks of the Fraser. This "strange new country" of people from around the world existed in Steveston for the duration of the salmon run, then disappeared, beginning to fade away completely in 1905 when a rail line to Vancouver made Steveston a nearby suburb of the city. Now fish landed in Steveston could be preserved in cold storages and shipped to luxury markets on the eastern seaboard in refrigerated rail cars in a matter of days. Steveston's isolation ended and its Nikkei community, despite continued reductions in its access to the Fraser fishery, found a measure of stability and prosperity. The unity that fishermen first glimpsed in 1900 became a reality in the 1950s. The Nikkei, when finally allowed to return to BC, joined the newly organized United Fishermen and Allied Workers' Union. The union and the Native Brotherhood of BC bargained fish prices and struck for recognition, winning both. Nikkei, Chinese and Indigenous people all finally won the right to vote. Recognition of Indigenous rights and title, however, remains a work in progress.

Yamazaki, Kelly and Rogers each represented much more what the province was becoming than what it had been. Yamazaki, the two-fisted intellectual with a gift for business, was as comfortable on the deck of a sealing schooner as he was in a newspaper office. He was just one of a generation of Nikkei leaders in Canada who left their native land at a time of breakneck modernization, someone with one foot in the era of the samurai and another in the world of trans-Pacific trade. Kelly was an industrial worker—in a sawmill town, a soap factory, the fishing industry and later in life as a logger—who took his place in the leadership of the Tsimshian after spending most of his life in Victoria, the province's second-largest city. And Rogers? He seems to have been that rarest of ideologues, someone who could put his beliefs into practice and convince hundreds of strangers to do the same.

It was their good fortune to come together momentarily, when the province's old system of political and economic power was giving way to a new one. In that moment, briefly, the province's most powerful men lost control. They didn't like what happened and tried to make sure it wouldn't happen again. But it could and it did.

ACKNOWLEDGEMENTS

A ny account of the Fraser River salmon strikes must stand
on the shoulders of Keith Ralston's remarkable 1965 MA
thesis, "The 1900 Strike of the Fraser River Fishermen." This
book is no exception. It was here that Frank Rogers's story
first assumed some tangible shape and the significance of the
strike was fully explored, although Rogers had been accorded
a heroic role in Bill Bennett's *Builders of British Columbia*,
written just thirty years after the events occurred.

Notwithstanding Ralston's meticulous account, based
on exhaustive research in the newspapers of the day, as well
as in federal fisheries records, he had no first-hand infor-
mation available from Nikkei sources or First Nations.
When I wrote my own history of the BC salmon fishery,
I had access to fragmentary translations of the Steveston
Fishermen's Benevolent Association history published in
Daphne Marlatt's *Steveston Recollected*. Those brief details

disclosed a very different perspective from the one reflected in news coverage of the dispute, which was all from the standpoint of the province's white majority. If Rogers had really achieved unity at all, I wondered, who on the Nikkei side had he worked with? Who among the First Nations leaders supported this strategy? News reports made it clear that George Kelly had been a leading voice of the Indigenous fleet, but the record was less clear on the Nikkei side.

Then the publication of Masako and Stan Fukawa's *Spirit of the Nikkei Fleet* offered a tantalizing new lead with a brief one-paragraph summary of the role of Yasushi Yamazaki. Soon after, I discovered Timothy Stielow's 2012 MA thesis "No Quarter Required: Japanese Experiences and Media Distortions in the Steveston Fishers' Strike of 1900." This work re-examines the news reports of the day and assesses them against a complete translation of the Dantai records for the first time. With these new materials in hand, I decided to look deeper into the lives of the three men most prominent in the leadership of the strike, each of whom became a leader in his own community in the years that followed. I am indebted to Bill McNulty, a Richmond city councillor and tireless chronicler of Steveston history, for a translation of the Steveston Japanese Fishermen's Benevolent Association history in his collection.

Since Ralston's pioneering work, labour researcher and writer Janet Nicol has done the most to flesh out Rogers's brief, mysterious passage through the province's history. I was able to add a few new facts to her work, but nothing of great significance, and I appreciated her willingness to urge me on.

George Kelly's life story proved equally elusive. I am indebted to Victor Kelly of Port Simpson, George Kelly's great-grandson, for reviewing my notes and confirming the facts that have come down to the current generation. The picture of George Kelly in the Nelson's Cornet Band is the only known surviving photograph. My thanks to Professor Steven Beda of the University of Washington for reviewing Viola Garfield's field notes of her interview with Kelly a few years before he died in Port Simpson. Her notes are held in the University of Washington Archives.

Yamazaki's story was preserved in *Footprints*, a tribute book of recollections by associates produced in his honour during the 1930s. A copy of this book is in the collection of the Nikkei National Museum and Cultural Centre in Burnaby. My deep appreciation goes to Masao and Stan Fukawa for their assistance in connecting me to Matsuki Masutani, of Denman Island, who translated the relevant portions of the book for my use. Yamazaki's personal story has many other remarkable chapters, including his newspaper campaigns against the prostitution of Nikkei women and his efforts to raise a battalion of Nikkei volunteers for the First World War, which deserve to be retold.

NOTES

1. Because many Japanese labourers from the latter half of the nineteenth century and first half of the twentieth were not necessarily Canadian citizens, the term *Nikkei* has been used throughout this text; it refers to people of Japanese ancestry living outside of Japan, whether they were Canadian citizens or not.

2. "Bound for South Africa," *Vancouver Daily World*, October 23, 1899, 2.

3. Ibid.

4. For the makeup of the volunteers see Ron LeBlanc, Keith Maxwell, Dwayne Snow, Kelly Deschenes, *Swift and Strong: A Pictorial History of the BC Regiment, Duke of Connaught's Own* (Vancouver: BC Regiment Museum Society, 2011), 13–23. R.A.J. McDonald puts the Asian population of Vancouver at 5 to 6 percent in 1900. See R.A.J. McDonald, "Working Class Vancouver, 1886–1914," in McDonald and Jean Barman, eds., *Vancouver Past: Essays in Social History*, Vancouver centennial issue of *BC Studies*, 41. The diversity of the fishing fleet was made plain in 1913 when it was found that of 1,430 licences on the Fraser that year, 660 were held by Nikkei, 230 by Indigenous people and the rest by 205 Canadians, 101 Scandinavians, 78 British, 35 Austrians, 28 Greeks, 23 Finns, 19 Italians, 17 Spaniards, eight Germans, ten French and seven Russians, as well as nine "indescribables." See also Geoff Meggs, *Salmon: The Decline of the Pacific Fishery* (Vancouver: Douglas and McIntyre, 1991), 93. Women made up about 13 percent of the workforce at that time.

5. Chuck Davis and Richard von Kleist, *Greater Vancouver Book: An Urban Encyclopaedia* (Surrey, BC: Linkman Press, 1977), 780. Also McDonald and others.

6. A.M. Stephen, "Vancouver," in *Vancouver Poetry*, Allan Safarik, ed. (Winlaw, BC: Polestar Press, 1986), 43.

7. Margaret Ormsby, *British Columbia: A History* (Vancouver: Macmillan Canada, 1958), 319.

8. Robert A.J. McDonald and Keith Ralston, "Francis Carter-Cotton," *Dictionary of Canadian Biography*, vol. XIV. http://www.biographi.ca/en/bio/carter_cotton_francis_lovett_14E.html.

9. J.A. Rea and Patricia Roy, "Joseph Martin," *Dictionary of Canadian Biography*, vol. XV. http://www.biographi.ca/en/bio/martin_joseph_15E.html.

10. Martin Robin, *The Rush for the Spoils: The Company Province, 1871–1933* (Toronto: McClelland and Stewart, 1972), 69–73; "What Martin Said," *Vancouver Daily World*, June 26, 1899, 3; "Slapped Martin's Face," *Vancouver Daily World*, June 22, 1899, 3.

11. R.A.J. McDonald, "He Thought He Was the Boss of Everything: Masculinity and Power in a Vancouver Family," *BC Studies*, no. 132 (Winter 2001/2002), 5–30.

12. Meggs, *Salmon*, 30 and 39–41; Percy Gladstone, "Native Indians and the Fishing Industry of British Columbia," *Canadian Journal of Economics and Political Science* 19, no. 1 (February 1953), 28–30.

13. McDonald, "He Thought He Was the Boss of Everything"; Meggs, *Salmon*, 25.

14. Fraser River Canners' Association minute book, June 26, 1900, 48. The opening price is not reported in the minutes, but is clear from subsequent events.

15. Meggs, *Salmon*, 27, 52.

16. Duncan Stacey, *Salmonopolis: The Steveston Story* (Vancouver: Harbour Publishing, 1991), 9–10.

17. Mary Cullen, *History of Fort Langley* (Ottawa: National Parks Branch, 1979); John Lutz, *Makuk: A New History of Aboriginal-White Relations* (Vancouver: UBC Press, 2008), 166.

18. Meggs, *Salmon*, 14–16.

19. Ibid., 54–58.

20. "Port Simpson Indians with A.E. Green planning for Dominion Day," *Vancouver Daily World*, June 30, 1900, 1; also *Vancouver Daily World*, June 30, 8.

21. "A Magnificent Celebration," *Vancouver Daily World*, July 3, 1900, 1.

22. James McDonald, "Images of the 19th Century Economy of the Tsimshian," in *The Tsimshian Images of the Past: Views from the Present*, Margaret Seguin, ed. (Vancouver: UBC Press, 1984), 42–53; Ken Campbell, "Hartley Bay: A History," in *The Tsimshian*, Seguin, 3–7; I.V.B. Johnson, "Legaic," in *Dictionary of Canadian Biography*, vol. XII. http://www.biographi.ca/en/bio/legaic_paul_12E.html.

23. Susan Neylan, *The Heavens Are Changing: Nineteenth-Century Protestant Missions and Tsimshian Christianity* (Montreal: McGill-Queen's University Press, 2003), 90.

24. Phylis Bowman, *Klondike of the Skeena!* (Chilliwack: Sunrise Printing, 1992); E.A. Harris, *Spokeshute: Skeena River Memory* (Victo-

ria: Orca Books Publishers, 1990); R. Geddies Large, *The Skeena: River of Destiny* (Sidney: Gray's Publishing, 1957, 1981); population notes from *Henderson's BC Gazetteer and Directory* (Vancouver, 1900), 275; Jean Friesen, "William Duncan," *Dictionary of Canadian Biography*, vol. XIV, http://www.biographi.ca/en/bio/duncan_william_14E.html; R.G. Large, *The Skeena: River of Destiny* (Vancouver: Mitchell Press, 1957), 38; Kenneth Campbell, *Persistence and Change: A History of the Ts'msyen Nation* (Prince Rupert: First Nation Education Council, 2005), 87–103.

25. Campbell, *Persistence and Change*, 99.

26. George Woodcock, *British Columbia: A History of the Province* (Vancouver: Douglas and McIntyre, 1992), 132; Peggy Brock, *The Many Voyages of Arthur Wellington Clah* (Vancouver: UBC Press, 2001), 206; Neylan, *The Heavens Are Changing*, 49.

27. Helen Meilleur, *A Pour of Rain: Stories from a West Coast Fort* (Vancouver: Raincoast, 2001), 40–46; Neylan, *The Heavens Are Changing*, 62.

28. Susan Neylan, "Here Comes the Band: Cultural Collaboration, Connective Traditions and the Aboriginal Brass Bands on British Columbia's North Coast," *BC Studies*, no. 152 (Winter 2006), 36.

29. The key facts of Kelly's life were set out in Viola Garfield's 1938 monograph "Tsimshian Clan and Society," *University of Washington Publications in Anthropology* 7, no. 3, 167–340. Garfield, who met Kelly in Port Simpson in 1932, the year before his death, was able to interview him.

30. Lutz, *Makuk*, 182.

31. A note on Diex's age: Alfred Dudoward's birthdate suggests Diex was at least in her teen years by that time, a fact that does not square with an 1891 census notation that she was forty-four years old, making her birth year closer to 1847. Nor does it fit with the age of forty-six she reported on her marriage certificate in 1887, suggesting she was born in 1841. In all likelihood, she was born in the 1830s, putting her in her mid-teens in 1850. (Felix Dudoward left Port Simpson in about 1859, perhaps for the gold rush, and his fate is unknown.)

32. Neylan, *The Heavens Are Changing*, 112–113.

33. Ibid., 112–115.

34. Neylan, "Here Comes the Band," 52.

35. Percy Gladstone, "Native Indians and the Fishing Industry of British Columbia," *Canadian Journal of Economics and Political Science* 19, no. 1 (February 1953), 28.

36. Meggs, *Salmon*, 40–43; Keith Ralston, "The 1900 Strike of the Fraser River Sockeye Fishermen," MA thesis, University of British Columbia, 1965, 48–68.

37. Rolf Knight, *Indians at Work: An Informal History of Native Labour in BC, 1858–1930* (Vancouver: New Star Books, 1996), 194–208; McDonald, *Making Vancouver*, 52–54.

38. Labour Day program, City of Vancouver Archives; Ross McCormack, *Reformers, Rebels and Revolutionaries: The Western Canadian Radical Movement, 1899–1919* (Toronto: University of Toronto Press, 1977).

39. J.E. Rea and Patricia Roy, "Joe Martin," *Dictionary of Canadian Biography*, vol. XV. http://www.biographi.ca/en/bio/martin_joseph_15E.html.

40. Ormsby, *British Columbia: A History*, 320–322.

41. Ormsby, *British Columbia: A History*, 305; Jean Barman, *The West Beyond the West* (Toronto: University of Toronto Press, 1991), 122–128.

42. J.R. Conley, "Class Conflict and Collective Action in the Working Class of Vancouver, BC, 1900–1919," PhD thesis, Carleton University, 1986, 122–126.

43. William Bennett, *Builders of British Columbia* (Vancouver, 1937); McCormack, *Reformers, Rebels and Revolutionaries*, 9; Mouat, "J.H. Watson," *Dictionary of Canadian Biography* XIII, http://www.biographi.ca/en/bio/watson_joseph_henry_13E.html.

44. Harold Griffin, *A Ripple, a Wave: The Story of Union Organization in the B.C. Fishing Industry* (Vancouver: Fisherman Publishing Society, 1974), 5.

45. Janet Nicol, "A Working Man's Dream," *BC History* 36, no. 2. I have supplemented Nicol's work with my own careful review of press reports. References to Watson are gleaned from Mouat, *Dictionary of Canadian Biography*.

46. Ronald Grantham, "Some Aspects of the Socialist Movement in British Columbia, 1898–1933," MA thesis, University of British Columbia, 1942, 11–15; Ross Johnson, "No Compromise, No Political Trading," PhD thesis, University of British Columbia, 1975, 11, 60.

47. A.R. McCormack, "Emergence of the Socialist Movement in British Columbia, *BC Studies* (Spring 1974), 9; "Not Socialists," *Vancouver Daily World*, January 16, 1903, 4.

48. The USLP soon changed once more into the Socialist Labor Party of British Columbia and went on to elect several MLAs.

49. Dennis Brown, personal communication, April 4, 2016.

50. Meggs, *Salmon*, 34–38.

51. *Province*, March 2, 1900; Ralston, *The 1900 Strike*, 97–100; "Analysis of Mongol Statistics," *The Independent*, April 21, 1900, 1.

52. Mitsuo Yesaki, *Sutebusuton: A Nikkei Village on the British Columbia Coast* (Vancouver: Peninsular Publishing, 2003), 9–13.

53. Bill McNulty, *Steveston: A Community History* (Richmond: Steveston Community Society, 2011), 6–12; Mitsuo Yesaki and Harold Steves, *Steveston Cannery Row: An Illustrated History* (Richmond: Peninsula Publishing Co., 2005), 9, 29–30.

54. Yesaki and Steves, *Steveston*.

55. Daphne Marlatt, *Steveston Recollected* (Victoria: Provincial Archives of BC, 1975), 5–10.

56. Takejiro Ooide, "Strife in Steveston," *Footprints: The Life of Yasushi Yamazaki* (Vancouver), 15–16. Excerpts from this tribute book, of which there is a copy in the Nikkei Museum and Archives, Burnaby, were translated for me by Matsuki Masutani in October 2014. The page numbers refer to his translation, not the original book.

57. "From Methodist Mission to Modern Hospital: The History of Steveston's Japanese Hospital 1895–1942," http://blogs.ubc.ca/nursing history/files/2014/02/rev-proof-19Nov-H.Vandenberg-NursingHistory-FINAL2.pdf; "Kanadà Dobo Hatten Taikan, Furoku," 1922. My copy on hand is a reproduction by Fuji Shyuppan, Tokyo, 111; Masako Fukawa and Stan Fukawa, *The Spirit of the Nikkei Fleet* (Madeira Park: Harbour Publishing, 2009), 73.

58. Timothy Stielow, "No Quarter Required: Japanese Experiences and Media Distortions in the Steveston Fishers' Strike of 1900," MA thesis, Simon Fraser University, 2012, 13.

59. Masako Fukawa and Stan Fukawa, *Spirit of the Nikkei Fleet*, 105.

60. Yidori and Midori Iwasaki, "Before Immigration," *Footprints*. The distance as the crow flies is 250 kilometres, so 400 kilometres sounds right given the long walk around to Kumagaya, but nine days seems very fast: 44 kilometres a day. Key facts are confirmed in Roy Ito, *Stories of My People: A Japanese Canadian Journal* (Hamilton: S-20 and Issei Veterans Association, 1994).

61. According to *Footprints*, Yamazaki returned to San Francisco in 1890. This would have made it impossible for him to observe the annexation of the Islands.

62. Yesaki, *Sutebusuton*, 5.

63. Peter Murray, *The Vagabond Fleet: A Chronicle of the North Pacific Sealing Schooner Trade* (Victoria: Sono Nis Press, 1988), 20–28.

64. J.H. Watson, "The Fishing Trouble," *Vancouver Daily World*, July 11, 1900, 3; "Fishermen's Strike," *News-Advertiser*, June 21, 1900, 6; Stielow, "No Quarter Required," 23–30; Ralston, *The 1900 Strike*, 110; "Papers Respecting the Strike among Fishermen on the Fraser River" (Victoria: BC legislature, 1900); Fraser River Canners' Association minute book.

65. Ooide, "Strife in Steveston," *Footprints*.

66. Ooide, *Footprints*, 18–20.

67. Ibid., 20.

68. Ibid., 18.

69. *The Independent*, April 28, 1900, 5, and May 12, 1900, 6; Ralston, *The 1900 Strike*, 100, 103.

70. Ooide, *Footprints*, 18. Ooide based his evaluation on his own experiences twenty years later trying to negotiate collaboration between Nikkei labourers and American Federation of Labour representatives.

71. Ooide's account of the strike itself contains some important errors, particularly his claim that there was a "Steveston Riot" requiring the

militia to be deployed after Japanese fishermen decided to fish for twenty-five cents. As a result, other aspects of his history must be treated with care. Nonetheless, his perspective on Yamazaki is insightful and revealing. See also British Columbia Sessional Papers, "Papers Respecting the Strike," 1900, clxxvii. (Sessional Papers are available at most major Canadian libraries; recent papers may be available online.)

72. Watson, "The Fishing Trouble," *Vancouver Daily World*, July 11, 1900, 6.

73. Ralston, *The 1900 Strike*, 110.

74. "Salmon Are Scarce, *Vancouver Daily World*, July 3, 1900, 3; Ralston, *The 1900 Strike*, 111–113; "Canners' Meeting, *Vancouver Daily World*, July 4, 1900, 8.

75. Marlatt, *Steveston Recollected*, 13.

76. Ralston, *The 1900 Strike*, 114.

77. Ibid.

78. Cited in Stielow, "No Quarter Required," 24–27.

79. Ibid., 29.

80. A subsequent press report says the whites used red flags and the Nikkei flew white ones (see Stielow, 43), but I have used Rogers's direct statement to the legislature committee. BC Sessional Papers, "Report of the Select Committee Appointed to Inquire into the Circumstances of Calling Out the Militia at Steveston," August 27, 1900, clxxvi.

81. "A Crisis Impending," *Province*, July 10, 1900. Cited by Stielow, 30.

82. BC Sessional Papers, 1900.

83. "Threw Out the Fish," *Vancouver Daily World*, July 11, 1900, 2; Documents relating to Fishermen's Strike at Steveston, BC Sessional Papers, 1900, mv; Ralston, *The 1900 Strike*, 116–121.

84. Cited in Stielow, "No Quarter Required," 38; "Capt. Anderson is Arrested," *Vancouver Daily World*, July 12, 1900, 1.

85. Cited in Stielow, "No Quarter Required," 30–32; "Procession tonight," *Vancouver Daily World*, July 14, 1900, 8.

86. Stielow, "No Quarter Required," 40; *Province*, July 1, 1900, 1.

87. "Fishermen Are Firm," *Province*, July 16, 1900, 3.

88. Stielow, "No Quarter Required," 47.

89. Stielow cites Teiji Kobayashi, *35 Nen Shi*, 81, 90; "The Fishermen's Strike," *News-Advertiser*, July 15, 1900, 8; for Campbell see BC Sessional Papers, "Calling Out the Militia at Steveston," 1900, clxvi.

90. Stielow, "No Quarter Required," 33–34; "Japs Own the River," *Vancouver Daily World*, July 9, 1900, 5.

91. "Trouble on the River," *New Westminster Columbian*, July 11, 1900, 2; "The Fisheries Trouble," *New Westminster Columbian*, July 12, 1900, 2; cited in Stielow, 44.

92. "New Westminster News," *Vancouver Daily World*, July 13, 1900, 3; "A Boat Cut in Two," *Vancouver Daily World*, July 16, 1900, 8.

93. *Independent*, July 28, 1900, 2; *News-Advertiser*, July 3, 1900, 8; *Province*, July 16, 1900, 3; *Vancouver Daily World*, July 17, 1900, 1; *Province*, July 19, 1900, 2; "New Westminster News," *Vancouver Daily World*, July 16, 1900, 3.

94. Kobayashi, cited in Stielow.

95. "Canners Will Confer," *Province*, July 17, 1900, 8; "Have Come Together: Canners and Fishermen in Amiable Conference," *Province*, July 18, 1900, 3; cited in Stielow, 51–52.

96. Ralston, *The 1900 Strike*, 125–127.

97. "Would Be a Loss over 20 Cents," *Vancouver Daily World*, July 20, 1900, 2.

98. BC Sessional Papers, "Calling Out the Militia at Steveston," 1900, clxxvii.

99. Special committee testimony of Campbell, clxxi.

100. Ralston, *The 1900 Strike*, 130; BC Sessional Papers, "Calling Out the Militia at Steveston," 1900, mx.

101. Ibid., cxli.

102. Fraser River Canners' Association minute book, July 21, 1900.

103. Ralston, *The 1900 Strike*, 132–133.

104. Teiji Kobayashi, 189; *New Westminster Columbian*, July 23, 1900; *Vancouver Daily World*, July 24, 1900, 1; Stielow, "No Quarter Required," 67.

105. Ibid., 70, citing Kobayashi; Griffin, *A Ripple, a Wave*.

106. Meggs, *Salmon*, 64; *Vancouver Daily World*, July 23, 1900, 3.

107. Stielow, "No Quarter Required," 65.

108. Marlatt, *Steveston Recollected*, 34.

109. BC Sessional Papers, July 19, 1900, xcii.

110. BC Sessional Papers, "Papers Respecting the Strike among Fishermen on the Fraser River," 1900, mv–mxiii.

111. Ralston, *The 1900 Strike*, 136 and ff.

112. Douglas Harker, "The Dukes: The Story of the Men Who Have Served in Peace and War with the BC Regiment (DCOR) 1883–1973," 27; Stielow, "No Quarter Required," 78–79.

113. Ralston, *The 1900 Strike*, 140.

114. Ibid., 141.

115. "All Quiet on the Fraser," *Vancouver Daily World*, July 23, 1900, 1, 8; BC Sessional Papers, "Report of the Special Legislative Committee," clxii.

116. Stielow, "No Quarter Required," 53–54.

117. Ralston, *The 1900 Strike*, 140–145; *Province*, July 24, 1900, 1; "All Quiet on the Fraser," *Vancouver Daily World*, July 25, 1900, 1, 8; BC Sessional Papers, 1900.

118. *News-Advertiser*, July 28, 5; Ralston, *The 1900 Strike*, 154–157; *The Independent*, July 14 and 21, 1.

119. Hotel reference from *Vancouver Daily World*, July 26, 1900.

120. *News-Advertiser*, July 29, 1900, 1; Ralston, *The 1900 Strike*, 160–165.

121. "Steveston Strike Settled," *New Westminster Columbian*, July 31, 1900, 1.

122. Ibid.

123. Marlatt, *Steveston Recollected*, 34.

124. BC Sessional Papers, 1900, xcii–xciii.

125. "Shall the Jap vote?" *Vancouver Daily World*, October 27, 1900, 1; BC Sessional Papers, "Report of the Delegation to Ottawa," 1900, dxliii, dxlv; Andrea Geiger-Adams, "Writing Racial Barrier into Law: Upholding BC's Denial of the Vote to Its Japanese Canadian Citizens, Homma v. Cunningham, 1902," in Louis Fiset and Gail Nomura, *Nikkei in the Pacific Northwest: Japanese Americans and Japanese Canadians in the Twentieth Century* (Seattle: Centre for the Study of the Pacific Northwest, University of Washington, 2005), 25–27.

126. Fraser River Canners' Association minute book.

127. *Independent*, August 25, 1900, 1.

128. Program in the collection of the Vancouver City Archives 1900–3: "Official Programme for Labor Day," September 3, 1900.

129. Yesaki, *Sutebusuton*, 36.

130. "The Royal City Honors Heroes," *Vancouver Daily World*, January 2, 1901, 1.

131. FRCA correspondence for 1901, from the author's collection.

132. Ooide, *Footprints*, 20.

133. "Social Life in Steveston," *Vancouver Daily World*, May 25, 1901, 1.

134. "Oppose Music Hall," *Vancouver Daily World*, July 5, 1901, 3.

135. Frank Rogers, "The Salmon Industry," *News-Advertiser*, April 13, 1901, 2.

136. "Critical Details about First Nations Meeting in Chilliwack," *Vancouver Daily World*, June 10, 1901, 1; see also *News-Advertiser*, June 11, 1901.

137. "Indians from across the Province," *Province*, June 7, 1901; "Men Insist on 15 Cents," *Vancouver Daily World*, June 10, 1901, 1.

138. "Chairman's Regret: Mr. Clute Gave a Strong Hint to the Canners," *Vancouver Daily World*, May 8, 1901, 2.

139. Royal Commission on Oriental Immigration, 385.

140. Ibid.

141. "Opposed to the Fishery Bill," *Vancouver Daily World*, May 3, 1901, 1.

142. "Salmon Canning," *Vancouver Daily World*, March 13, 1901, 2; "Men and Canners Confer," *Vancouver Daily World*, July 17, 1901, 1; *Province*, June 17, 1901, 1.

143. Meggs, *Salmon*, 87.

144. Burdis to FRCA, June 27, 1901. A copy of this note is in the possession of the author.

145. "Nikkei accept offer," *Colonist*, June 20, 1901, 1; "Nikkei to Accept 12.5 Cents," *Vancouver Daily World*, June 20, 1901, 1.

146. "Nikkei Accept Offer," *Colonist*, June 20, 1901, 1; "Fishermen's Meeting," *Vancouver Daily World*, June 27, 1901, 2.

147. "Fishermen's Meeting," *Vancouver Daily World*, June 25, 1901, 1.

148. "Endorsed the Men: Fishermen's Mass Meeting in the City Hall," *Vancouver Daily World*, June 27, 1901, 2; "Mass Meeting," *News-Advertiser*, June 26, 1901; Meggs, *Salmon*, 67.

149. "The Strike on CPR, Trackmen in British Columbia Write More Letters," *Vancouver Daily World*, June 26, 1901, 1.

150. "Midnight Set as Deadline after Prolonged Meeting," *News-Advertiser*, June 30, 1901.

151. "Nikkei Fishing," *Colonist*, July 7, 1901, 1.

152. Ooide, *Footprints*, 20.

153. "Whites Determined to Run Out Nikkei," *Anaconda Standard*, July 11, 1901, 1.

154. "Japs Have the River," *Vancouver Daily World*, July 8, 1901, 1.

155. "Captive Japs Spirited Away," *Province*, July 11, 1901, 1.

156. All from Ooide, *Footprints*, and Dantai, *35 Years*.

157. "Arrest of Frank Rogers," IPSFC clipping book, 84; "Arrest of a Fisherman Leader," *Vancouver Daily World*, July 12, 1901, 1; "36 Japs Marooned," *Province*, July 12, 1901, 1. (This is Brown's scoop.)

158. Unidentified clip, IPSFC clipping book.

159. "Arrest of Frank Rogers," IPSFC clipping book, 84; "Arrest of a Fisherman Leader," *Vancouver Daily World*, July 12, 1901, 1; "36 Japs Marooned," *Province*, July 12, 1901, 1. (This is Brown's scoop.)

160. Unidentified clip, IPSFC clipping book, 74–79. The clippings are seldom identifiable as those of a specific newspaper.

161. IPSFC clipping book, 80–88.

162. "Quiet on the Fraser," IPSFC clipping book, 97.

163. *The Colonist*, July 17, 1901; "Hated to Tell, but He Had To," *Vancouver Daily World*, July 17, 1901, 1.

164. "Fishermen Accusers Now," *Province*, July 17, 1901, 1; IPSFC clipping book, 104; "Hated to Tell, but He Had To," *Vancouver Daily World*, July 17, 1901, 1.

165. "Arrest of a Fisherman Leader," *Vancouver Daily World*, July 12, 1901, 1.

166. "The Fishermen Met," *Vancouver Daily World*, July 15, 1901, 5.

167. "Salmon Strike Is Settled," *Province*, July 1, 1901, 1; "Indians Preparing to Fish," *Vancouver Daily World*, July 20, 1901, 10; "Strike Ended," *Vancouver Daily World*, July 19, 1901, 1; Meggs, *Salmon*, 69.

168. "Thousands of Dead and Decaying Salmon Polluting the River," *Vancouver Daily World*, August 12, 1901, 1.

169. Meggs, *Salmon*, 70.

170. The guarantors included Alexander Bruce, ex-alderman of Ward 5; John Charles Marshall, a plumber; Colin MacKinnon, owner of the Terminus Hotel; Charles Woodward, Westminster Avenue merchant and mayoral candidate; and Charles Wellig, a co-accused who had also been acquitted.

171. Various *Vancouver Daily World* stories, November 9, 1901, 6; November 19, 1901, 1.

172. Andrea Geiger-Adams, "Writing Racial Barrier into Law," 27–30, in Louis Fiset and Gail Nomura, *Nikkei in the Pacific Northwest: Japanese Americans and Japanese Canadians in the Twentieth Century* (Seattle: Centre for the Study of Pacific Northwest, University of Washington, 2005).

173. "Welcome to the West: Our Future King and Queen Receive the Homage of this Magic City," *Vancouver Daily World*, September 30, 1901, 1.

174. *Swift and Strong*, 16–23; "Soldiers Depart, Coast Contingent Cheered on Their Way," *Vancouver Daily World*, October 23, 1899, 8.

175. R.A.J. McDonald, "He Thought He Was the Boss of Everything," *BC Studies*, no. 132 (Winter 2001/2002), 5–30.

176. Meggs, *Salmon*, 70–72.

177. *Yosemite* (sidewheeler), Wikipedia, https://en.wikipedia.org/wiki/Yosemite_(sidewheeler).

178. The details of the UBRE strike are based for the most part on J. Hugh Tuck, "The United Brotherhood of Railway Employees in Western Canada, 1898–1905," *Labour Le Travail* (Spring 1983), 63–88.

179. "McGregor Was Acquitted This Afternoon," *Province*, May 7, 1903, 1.

180. "Mr. Rogers Had No Possible Chance," *Vancouver Daily World*, April 16, 1903, 1. The entire passage reads: "Better be with the dead/ Whom we, to gain our peace, have sent to peace,/ Than on the torture of the mind to lie/ In restless ecstasy. Duncan is in his grave;/ After life's fitful fever he sleeps well."

181. Ernest Burns, "Frank Rogers," *Vancouver Daily World*, April 8, 1911, 34.

182. The 1891 census shows Kelly, Lucy and their children living in Victoria, where Kelly worked in the soap factory. Both children were born in the United States.

183. Carol Cooper writes: "Because Nisga'a and Tsimshian children continued to derive their clan affiliation and status from their mothers, the fact that the child was of mixed descent appeared to have no negative bearing upon his or her status within the tribe. Tsimshian oral traditions claim that fairness of skin and hair were looked upon with favour and that a child of mixed descent 'in the village gets every thought.'" She adds that "Mixed-blood offspring of high-ranking women often played prominent

roles in the community throughout the fur trade and mission periods. Two such men, Alfred Dudoward (Skagwait) and David Swanson were among the highest-ranking chiefs at Port Simpson in 1900 and were frequently called upon by their tribes to represent them in land negotiations and other meetings with the governmental authorities." Carol Cooper, "Native Women of the Northern Pacific Coast: An Historical Perspective, 1830–1900," *Journal of Canadian Studies* 27, no. 4 (1991–1993), 44–75.

184.   Viola Garfield papers, 2027-001, Box 7, Folder 4, pp. 101–110, July 10, 1932.

185.   Peggy Brock, *The Many Voyages of Arthur Wellington Clah: A Tsimshian Man on the Pacific Northwest Coast* (Vancouver: UBC Press, 2011), 195–196, 204–209. Brock says Kelly did not die until 1938, but the BC Death Index shows he died in 1933 at the age of seventy-six. If he was indeed seventy-six, he must have been born in 1857. That would put his first marriage at the age of nineteen. Also Garfield, 184.

186.   Neylan, *Here Comes the Band*, 58.

187.   Ooide, *Footprints*.

188.   Aya Fujiwara, "The Myth of the Emperor and the Yamato Race: The Role of the Tairiku Nippo in the Promotion of Japanese-Canadian Transnational Ethnic Identity in the 1920s and 1930s." *Journal of the Canadian Historical Association* 21, no. 1 (2010), p. 37–58, especially 40.

189.   Ito, *Stories of My People*, 76–78.

190.   Miyoko Kudō, *Kiiroi Heishi Tachi (Yellow Soldiers)* (Tokyo: Kobunsha, 1983), from a translation summary prepared by Stan Fukawa.

191.   Ibid.

192.   "Prominent Men Become Citizens of the Empire," *Vancouver Daily World*, January 8, 1916, 1; "Editor Host to Local Japanese," *Vancouver Daily World*, July 2, 1917, 14.

193.   Ormsby, *British Columbia: A History*, 331–336; Robin, *The Rush for the Spoils*, 82–86.

194.   Paul Tennant, *Aboriginal People and Politics: The Indian Land Question in BC, 1849–1989* (Vancouver: UBC Press, 1990), 108–124.

INDEX

Page numbers in **bold** refer to images in the photo insert.